PUBLIC SPENDING POLICIES IN LATIN AMERICA AND THE CARIBBEAN

Scan the QR code to see all titles in this series.

Latin American Development Forum

PUBLIC SPENDING POLICIES IN LATIN AMERICA AND THE CARIBBEAN

When Cyclicality Meets Rigidities

Daniel Riera-Crichton and
Guillermo Vuletin

 WORLD BANK GROUP

ISBN (paper): 978-1-4648-2069-4
ISBN (electronic): 978-1-4648-2070-0
DOI: 10.1596/978-1-4648-2069-4

Cover design: Melina Rose Yingling / World Bank.

Library of Congress Control Number: 2024910799

Latin American Development Forum Series

This series was created in 2003 to promote debate, disseminate information and analysis, and convey the excitement and complexity of the most topical issues in economic and social development in Latin America and the Caribbean. It is sponsored by the Inter-American Development Bank, the United Nations Economic Commission for Latin America and the Caribbean, and the World Bank, and represents the highest quality in each institution's research and activity output. Titles in the series have been selected for their relevance to the academic community, policy makers, researchers, and interested readers, and have been subjected to rigorous anonymous peer review prior to publication.

Advisory Committee Members

Jose Manuel Salazar Xirinachs, Executive Secretary, Economic Commission for Latin America and the Caribbean, United Nations

Raquel Artecona, Economic Affairs Officer, Economic Commission for Latin America and the Caribbean, United Nations

Eric Parrado, Chief Economist and General Manager, Research Department, Inter-American Development Bank

Carlos Scartascini, Head, Development Research Group, Inter-American Development Bank

William Maloney, Chief Economist of the Latin America and the Caribbean Region, World Bank

Marcela Meléndez, Deputy Chief Economist of the Latin America and the Caribbean Region, World Bank

Roberto Rigobon, Professor of Applied Economics, Sloan School of Management, Massachusetts Institute of Technology

Ernesto Talvi, Senior Analyst at the Elcano Royal Institute

Andrés Velasco, Dean of the School of Public Policy at the London School of Economics and Political Science

Titles in the Latin American Development Forum Series

New Century, Old Disparities: Gaps in Ethnic and Gender Earnings in Latin America and the Caribbean (2012) by Hugo Ñopo

Does What You Export Matter? In Search of Empirical Guidance for Industrial Policies (2012) by Daniel Lederman and William F. Maloney

From Right to Reality: Incentives, Labor Markets, and the Challenge of Achieving Universal Social Protection in Latin America and the Caribbean (2012) by Helena Ribe, David Robalino, and Ian Walker

Breeding Latin American Tigers: Operational Principles for Rehabilitating Industrial Policies (2011) by Robert Devlin and Graciela Moguillansky

New Policies for Mandatory Defined Contribution Pensions: Industrial Organization Models and Investment Products (2010) by Gregorio Impavido, Esperanza Lasagabaster, and Manuel García-Huitrón

The Quality of Life in Latin American Cities: Markets and Perception (2010) by Eduardo Lora, Andrew Powell, Bernard M. S. van Praag, and Pablo Sanguinetti, editors

Discrimination in Latin America: An Economic Perspective (2010) by Hugo Ñopo, Alberto Chong, and Andrea Moro, editors

The Promise of Early Childhood Development in Latin America and the Caribbean (2010) by Emiliana Vegas and Lucrecia Santibáñez

Job Creation in Latin America and the Caribbean: Trends and Policy Challenges (2009) by Carmen Pagés, Gaëlle Pierre, and Stefano Scarpetta

China's and India's Challenge to Latin America: Opportunity or Threat? (2009) by Daniel Lederman, Marcelo Olarreaga, and Guillermo E. Perry, editors

Does the Investment Climate Matter? Microeconomic Foundations of Growth in Latin America (2009) by Pablo Fajnzylber, Jose Luis Guasch, and J. Humberto López, editors

Measuring Inequality of Opportunities in Latin America and the Caribbean (2009) by Ricardo Paes de Barros, Francisco H. G. Ferreira, José R. Molinas Vega, and Jaime Saavedra Chanduvi

The Impact of Private Sector Participation in Infrastructure: Lights, Shadows, and the Road Ahead (2008) by Luis Andres, Vivien Foster, Jose Luis Guasch, and Thomas Haven

Remittances and Development: Lessons from Latin America (2008) by Pablo Fajnzylber and J. Humberto López, editors

Fiscal Policy, Stabilization, and Growth: Prudence or Abstinence? (2007) by Guillermo Perry, Luis Servén, and Rodrigo Suescún, editors

Raising Student Learning in Latin America: Challenges for the 21st Century (2007) by Emiliana Vegas and Jenny Petrow

Investor Protection and Corporate Governance: Firm-Level Evidence across Latin America (2007) by Alberto Chong and Florencio López-de-Silanes, editors

Natural Resources: Neither Curse nor Destiny (2007) by Daniel Lederman and William F. Maloney, editors

The State of State Reform in Latin America (2006) by Eduardo Lora, editor

Emerging Capital Markets and Globalization: The Latin American Experience (2006) by Augusto de la Torre and Sergio L. Schmukler

Beyond Survival: Protecting Households from Health Shocks in Latin America (2006) by Cristian C. Baeza and Truman G. Packard

Beyond Reforms: Structural Dynamics and Macroeconomic Vulnerability (2005) by José Antonio Ocampo, editor

Privatization in Latin America: Myths and Reality (2005) by Alberto Chong and Florencio López-de-Silanes, editors

Keeping the Promise of Social Security in Latin America (2004) by Indermit S. Gill, Truman G. Packard, and Juan Yermo

Lessons from NAFTA for Latin America and the Caribbean (2004) by Daniel Lederman, William F. Maloney, and Luis Servén

The Limits of Stabilization: Infrastructure, Public Deficits, and Growth in Latin America (2003) by William Easterly and Luis Servén, editors

Globalization and Development: A Latin American and Caribbean Perspective (2003) by José Antonio Ocampo and Juan Martin, editors

Is Geography Destiny? Lessons from Latin America (2003) by John Luke Gallup, Alejandro Gaviria, Eduardo Lora Guasch, Thomas Haven, and Vivien Foster

All books in the Latin American Development Forum series are available for free at https://openknowledge.worldbank.org/handle/10986/2167.

Contents

Figures

Maps

Tables

Acknowledgments

The study described in this report was led by Daniel Riera-Crichton, previously a senior economist at the World Bank and currently a professor of economics at Bates College, and Guillermo Vuletin, a senior economist at the World Bank. It was conducted under the general guidance of William F. Maloney, chief economist, Latin America and the Caribbean Region (LCR). During the concept note stage, the report benefited from the guidance of Martin Rama and Carlos Végh, both former LCR chief economists.

The report was written by Daniel Riera-Crichton and Guillermo Vuletin with input from a team that included José Andrée Camarena (World Bank), Jessica Bracco (Universidad Nacional de La Plata), Luciana Galeano (University of Michigan), Pedro Juarros (International Monetary Fund), Carlos Végh (Johns Hopkins University), and Lucila Venturi (Harvard University).

Special thanks to Pilar Ruiz (World Bank), who provided invaluable research and editorial support throughout the preparation of the study.

Several distinguished peer reviewers provided excellent advice. Jorge Araujo, Doerte Doemeland, Ayhan Kose, Aart Kraay, Franziska Lieselotte Ohnsorge, and Norman Loayza—all at the World Bank—provided guidance and invaluable comments on the concept note and decision drafts. Appreciation is extended to Carlos Felipe Jaramillo, William Maloney, and Seynabou Sakho for their useful comments during our decision meeting. We also thank two anonymous referees at the Latin American Development Forum for their insightful comments.

The team was fortunate to receive support from many experts and colleagues: Pierre Bachas (World Bank), Cesar Calderon (World Bank), Roberto N. Fattal Jaef (World Bank), Alejandro Izquierdo (Inter-American Development Bank), Graciela Kaminsky (George Washington University), Ruy Lama (International Monetary Fund), Juan Pablo Medina (Universidad Adolfo Ibáñez), Steven Pennings (World Bank), Carola Pessino (Inter-American Development Bank), and Jorge Puig (Universidad Nacional de La Plata).

During its final stages, the study benefited from the comments of participants in the launch of the report at the Latin American and Caribbean Economic Association conference in Lima, Peru. Carlos Végh provided an in-depth discussion of the report.

Publication of the report was overseen and carried out by Jewel McFadden (acquisitions editor). Caroline Polk was production editor, Kathie Porta Baker was copy editor, and Talia Greenberg Hudgins was proofreader. Information officers in the Cartography Unit of the World Bank prepared the final versions of some of the maps featured in the book. Finally, Jacqueline Larrabure Rivero provided excellent administrative support.

Although the guidance of the reviewers, advisers, and discussants was invaluable, any remaining errors, omissions, or interpretations are those of the authors.

About the Authors

Daniel Riera-Crichton is a professor of economics at Bates College. He is also a research associate at the Globalization Institute at the Federal Reserve Bank of Dallas and a research fellow at the Santa Cruz Institute for International Economics. Prior to his current position, Daniel was a senior economist at the Office of the Chief Economist for Latin America and the Caribbean of the World Bank. His research agenda addresses issues of persistent current account imbalances, international financial integration, commodity price shocks, real exchange rates, international reserves, and fiscal policy. Riera-Crichton's work has been published in the *Journal of Monetary Economics, Review of Economics and Statistics, Journal of International Economics, Journal of Development Economics,* and *Journal of International Money and Finance,* as well as in other journals. His research has been featured in popular media such as *The Washington Post, Chicago Tribune, Tampa Bay Times, Mother Jones,* and others, as well as policy forums such as Brookings Up Front, World Economic Forum, and VoxEU. Riera-Crichton holds a PhD in economics from the University of California, Santa Cruz; an MA from Universitat Pompeu Fabra; and a BA from Universitat Autónoma de Barcelona.

Guillermo Vuletin is a senior economist at the Office of the Chief Economist for Latin America and the Caribbean of the World Bank. He is also an associate editor of *Economía LACEA Journal,* the journal of the Latin American and Caribbean Economic Association. Before joining the World Bank, he was a lead economist at the Research Department of the Inter-American Development Bank. His research focuses on fiscal and monetary policies, with a particular interest in macroeconomic policy in low- and middle-income countries. Vuletin's work has been published in the *Journal of Monetary Economics, Journal of International Economics, American Economic Journal: Economic Policy,* and *Journal of Development Economics,* as well as in other journals. His research has been featured in prominent media outlets, such as *The Economist, The Wall Street Journal, Financial Times, The Washington Post,* and other international and regional newspapers. Vuletin holds a PhD in economics from the University of Maryland and an undergraduate degree and an MA in economics from the Universidad Nacional de La Plata, La Plata, Argentina.

Executive Summary

MAIN MESSAGES

- Unlike high-income economies, low- and middle-income markets exhibit a unique pattern in which short-term economic boosts trigger long-term spending commitments, leading to fiscal rigidity amid cyclical conditions.
- In low- and middle-income markets, public spending tends to be semiprocyclical during economic booms, contrary to traditional Keynesian theory, exacerbating macroeconomic volatility and hindering quality public investment.
- Addressing the challenge of mismatched spending commitments and economic cycles requires a departure from traditional macroeconomic approaches, and policy makers are urged to implement innovative fiscal rules and efficient public investment strategies.
- In the absence of effective automatic stabilizers such as unemployment insurance because of high informality rates, low- and middle-income markets rely on rigid social transfer programs, further complicating fiscal dynamics and economic recovery.
- Uncovering anomalies in low- and middle-income markets' fiscal policies unveils the need for nuanced approaches beyond conventional remedies, emphasizing the importance of balancing short-term stability with long-term economic sustainability.

Thinking about public spending in high-income economies falls broadly into two categories. On the one hand, Keynesian-type spending to moderate downturns in the business cycle generally works through automatic stabilizers such as unemployment insurance and discretionary injections of public investment that ensure against large drops in private consumption and investment, respectively. In other words, short-run spending policies are used to deal with short-run economic problems. On the other hand, public finance microeconomists have studied the structural links relating public spending to secular questions such as the optimal size of the government and the efficient provision of public goods such as education, health, or public safety.

This report shows that public spending policies in low- and middle-income markets do not follow the same canons observed in their high-income counterparts. At the core of these differences is the fact that, because of a variety of structural differences, low- and middle-income markets make long-term (rigid) public spending commitments based on short-run (cyclical) economic conditions. These maturity mismatches in public spending policy contribute to greater difficulties in resolving fiscal disequilibria and force compositional changes in public spending that undermine the necessary public sector contributions to economic growth.

Departing from the traditional approach in the macroeconomic literature, we break apart the behavior of overall primary spending, "big G," and study the cyclical behavior of its components. Going beyond big G allows us to gain a better understanding of how well-known structural problems in low- and middle-income markets lead to severe asymmetries across the business cycle in the behavior of certain components of public spending. Not only do the resulting dynamics exacerbate macroeconomic volatility instead of moderating it, but they also have first-order negative impacts on the provision of public investment. In particular, we identify three pervasive spending policy anomalies in low- and middle-income markets related to rigid spending along the business cycle that are virtually absent in high-income economies.

First, counter to standard Keynesian prescriptions, low- and middle-income markets' public spending is semiprocyclical during economic booms. That is, in good times, when economic activity and revenues are temporarily booming, governments' public spending increases. As the literature has documented, this is partially due to increased access to borrowing and partially due to political pressures to redress long-standing social shortfalls that become harder to resist. Spending is semiprocyclical because much of the spending undertaken during good times is of a downwardly rigid nature and hence does not contract during downturns. Teachers are hired, hospitals are staffed, and constituencies are established. International financial institutions and governments often try to ring-fence such expenditures to protect vulnerable populations during downturns. However well intentioned, the net effect not only exacerbates macroeconomic volatility but also degrades the quality of public investment.

Although fully acknowledging the need to redress long-standing shortfalls in the provision of public goods in low- and middle-income markets, public finance and adjustment cost theory advise that desired increases in spending on health or education should nonetheless be smooth rather than increase spasmodically over the business cycle. There are, broadly speaking, adjustment costs or time to build. Rapidly hiring teachers during an upturn when cash-flush may not permit careful vetting or drafting from successive graduate training classes. Nor may there be time to learn from previous experience in building new medical centers. A growing number of studies precisely document the poor quality of much of public spending, which, in turn, jeopardizes the future returns required to cover today's investments.

Second, large levels of labor market informality in low- and middle-income markets make automatic stabilizers such as unemployment insurance impractical; hence, governments use public employment and social transfer programs to support incomes in downturns. Such programs are typically designed to address structural poverty issues, and consequently their use in a cyclical context already implies design inefficiencies to add to the intermittent increases in the provision of public goods discussed earlier. More germane to the present discussion, they are also downwardly rigid by nature because they lack clear termination criteria, and governments are typically reluctant or politically incapable of winding them down as economies recover.

Downward rigidities in public consumption during bad times and social transfers in good times build in something of a ratchet effect that, if financed by increased debt or tax revenues, would lead to ever-larger governments. In practice, countervailing forces, in the form of limited local taste for taxation and access to credit or other resources, lead governments to reach a steady-state government size that varies across the region. We show some countries to be above their spending predictions, based on their level of development, and in some cases below them.

In the end, however, the downward rigidity of some components of spending and the demands of fiscal sustainability imply that something has to give, and this leads to large changes in the composition of spending, which, in turn, have acute immediate welfare and long-term growth consequences. Particularly prevalent are biases against pension benefits and public investment, two of the few categories of public spending that wind up being flexible and discretionary.

Uncovering these anomalies allows us to provide policy prescriptions that go beyond the traditional ones addressing the original sins (increase financial depth, improve institutional quality, and lower labor market informality, among other recommendations) and could be helpful for policy makers in the short run. Some examples may be setting up fiscal rules to tame overspending in the good times, improve the quality and efficiency of public goods, and set up mechanisms to cut social and employment programs for those who move out of poverty during good times without incentivizing informality or protecting public investment during economic busts.

Chapter 1 of the report discusses differences in the evolution of the size and composition of public spending between high-income and low- and middle-income nations. These differences are cause and effect of the public spending anomalies highlighted in this study. The semiprocyclical behavior of public consumption in low- and middle-income markets during economic booms and its potential macroeconomic consequences are discussed in chapter 2. Chapter 3 studies the semicountercyclical behavior of social transfers in low- and middle-income markets during economic recessions, identifying potential roots of this behavior and its macroeconomic consequences. Chapter 4 combines the observations of the previous chapters to explain why low- and middle-income markets are forced to adjust via social security and public investment, thus creating immediate social costs as well as worsening long-run economic prospects. Finally, chapter 5 concludes with some relevant policy considerations.

Abbreviations

AE	Auxílio Emergencial
BBRs	budget balance rules
CCTs	conditional cash transfers
DR	debt rules
ER	expenditure rules
ESCS	economic, social, and cultural status
GDP	gross domestic product
HtM	hand to mouth
IMF	International Monetary Fund
LAC	Latin America and the Caribbean
NFPS	nonfinancial public sector
OECD	Organisation for Economic Co-operation and Development
PISA	Programme for International Student Assessment
p.p.	percentage point
PPI	Private Participation in Infrastructure
SNAP	Supplemental Nutrition Assistance Program
STMs	social transfer multipliers
SVAR	structural vector autoregression
TANK	two-agent new Keynesian
UI	unemployment insurance

1

Public Spending 101: Low- and Middle-Income Markets Are Different

Size and Evolution of Public Spending

The direct roles of the public sector in the economy are typically considered to be twofold. First, governments can lower economic uncertainty by building resilience against negative economic shocks using countercyclical policies typically conducted through automatic stabilizers, such as unemployment insurance or discretionary spending in the form of public investment. Second, through the provision of public goods such as education, health, justice, and public safety, among others, governments enhance productivity and the well-being of citizens while internalizing the distortionary implications of the taxation needed to finance government spending (for example, income elasticity of taxation or distributional issues associated with the size of tax rates and their progressivity). On the social front, the public sector can adopt a redistributive role in spending on social insurance as well as on direct transfers to the public.

The number of resources with which countries decide to endow the public sector depends on several idiosyncratic cultural, political, and economic factors. At the core of what determines the size of the government lies a key economic trade-off. On the one hand, small governments minimize potential costs associated with crowding out the private sector. In this sense, because government spending needs to be financed with current or future taxes, households trying to smooth their consumption paths will increase their savings to pay for such taxes, thus decreasing private consumption. Financing spending via borrowing will increase competition for available funds in the economy and may push private investors out of the market. This means that, by and large, if government spending and borrowing go up, private spending and borrowing tend to go down.[1] On the other hand, governments deliver underprovided public goods, create economies of scale, and provide infrastructural development that is, in many instances, a required precursor to private investment. Aschauer (1989) shows how infrastructure can "crowd in" private investment by increasing productivity. Greene and Villanueva (1991), Easterly and Rebelo (1993), and Erden and Holcombe (2005) show that public investment leads to private capital accumulation in low- and middle-income countries. Governments can also play a redistributive role by targeting reductions in inequality and providing resources for those who are most vulnerable.

Empirical studies show that countries with a large population tend to have relatively smaller governments (and therefore lower taxes) because they benefit from economies of scale in the provision of public goods (see Alesina and Wacziarg 1998). Also, more open countries (that is, those with higher shares of international trade relative to their economic size) are, generally, subject to more shocks and may therefore need larger governments (see Rodrik 1998).[2] Lamartina and Zaghini (2011) show that underdeveloped countries tend to have higher elasticities in public spending on development as they converge with high-income counterparts. On the financing side, low- and middle-income countries tend to rely heavily on international trade taxes, whereas income taxes are only important in high-income economies. These revenue constraints may provide a further link between the size of the public sector and economic development (see Easterly and Rebelo 1993). On the institutional front, Stein, Talvi, and Grisanti (1998) find evidence that electoral systems characterized by a large degree of proportionality tend to have larger governments because voters have an incentive to elect representatives more prone to transfer spending in proportional systems (see also Milesi-Ferretti, Perotti, and Rostagno 2002). Persson and Tabellini (1999) find that the size of governments is smaller under presidential as opposed to parliamentarian regimes.

Political science literature, mostly based on Organisation for Economic Co-operation and Development (OECD) countries, has also found evidence of larger public sectors under left-leaning governments (see Blais, Blake, and Dion 1996; Cusack, Notermans, and Rein 1989; Roubini and Sachs 1989a; and Schmidt 2002, among others) as well as under powerful unions (see Alvarez, Garrett, and Lange 1991; Garrett 1998; Iversen and Cusack 2000). Constraints faced by parties in coalition and minority governments also lead to larger governments (see Blais, Blake, and Dion 1993, 1996; De Haan and Sturm 1994, 1997). Roubini and Sachs (1989b) argue that the power dispersion in coalition and minority governments leads to increased logrolling (that is, trading support for one issue or piece of legislation in exchange for another's support) among parties that would eventually result in a higher share of public spending in the economy. More recently, empirical studies have looked at the interplay of factors influencing the supply and demand of public goods. Mahdavi (2008) examined a diverse array of explanatory variables affecting the demand for public goods in low- and middle-income countries, including population structure and education. The supply side of the equation was characterized by factors such as the level of corruption, political regime, and proxies reflecting the costs of tax collection. Bird, Martinez-Vazquez, and Torgler (2014) put a particular emphasis on the quality of institutions. Their findings indicated that dependable political institutions enhance the supply of public goods, thereby increasing the willingness of individuals to contribute through taxes. In a recent theoretical article,

Fedotenkov and Idrisov (2021) show that the size of the public sector may depend on the median voter's income, population size, costs associated with paying taxes, and quality of institutions, all of which reflect the costs of provisioning public goods.

Since the early twentieth century, studies have associated the growth of public spending with economic development. In their highly influential papers, Wagner (1893) and, later, Peacock and Wiseman (1961, 1979) discuss a shift from private to public sector activity in the form of provision of public goods such as education, health, justice, and public safety, among others, as countries industrialize.[3] This relationship, better known as Wagner's law, is based on voters demanding more social services and risk-mitigating expenditures as their income grows. The increase in state expenditure is needed because of the increase in the state's social activities, higher number of administrative and protective actions, and improvement in the welfare functions (see Musgrave 1959).

Examples of newly funded programs include retirement insurance, natural disaster aid, environmental protection programs, and science and technology grants. Governments also pay larger interest bills as their debt grows over time. Additionally, Wagner (1893) argued that the risk of private monopolies growing from technological progress would require governments to engage in redistributive efforts.

Figure 1.1 shows data evidence of the effectiveness of Wagner's law in a sample of countries from 1980 to 2019. Although a fair amount of dispersion is related to the existence of other important roots of public spending, as described earlier, the scatterplot shows how the share of the public sector in the economy grows with national income.

Despite this evidence, the time series of public spending in high-income and low- and middle-income countries shows very different patterns. As shown in figure 1.2, the size of the public sector in high-income economies has increased significantly over the past century from 10 percent in 1900 to more than 44 percent in 2015. Meanwhile, low- and middle-income markets have also steadily increased over the past century but to a lower level of around 32 percent on average by 2015.[4]

Although the path of public spending in high-income economies mostly followed their economic development, instead of following output trends smoothly, as predicted by Wagner's law, public spending since the late 1800s seems to be generated by a step function. To explain the steps in the spending function, Peacock and Wiseman (1961, 1979) proposed a theory based on large disturbances that cause major shifts in public expenditure levels (for example, armed conflicts). These shifts require revenue increases that would cause short-lived voter displeasure. Once citizens adjust their tolerance to the new levels of taxation, the new level of public expenditure will be cemented. This theory fits well the profile of high-income economies for which significant jumps in the level of public expenditure appear after each world war and after the global oil shocks in the 1970s.[5]

Although low- and middle-income countries did experience conflict and natural disasters that required rebuilding efforts by the public sector during the past century, these countries were generally spared from the devastating effects of the two world wars that drove large jumps in public spending across high-income economies. Instead, ratchet effects in low- and middle-income markets are typically originated along the business

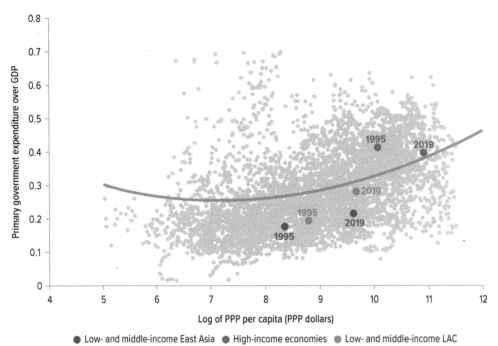

Source: Original calculations for this publication based on data from the International Monetary Fund World Economic Outlook database (various years).
Note: Blue dots represent country-year data points for all countries where data is available. Low- and middle-income markets in Latin America and East Asia, as well as high-income countries, are highlighted because of their evolution from 1995 to 2019. GDP = gross domestic product; LAC = Latin America and the Caribbean; PPP = purchasing power parity. Refer to Annex 1A for classifications of low-, middle-, and high-income economies.

FIGURE 1.2: Size of Government in a World Historical Perspective

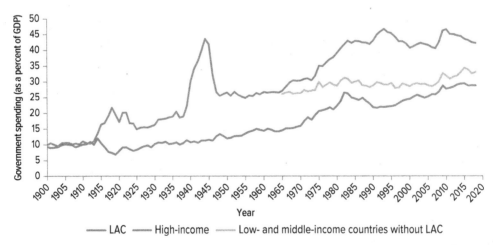

Source: Original calculations based on a novel historical dataset of 196 countries since their independence or consolidation.
Note: For each group, the ratio of general government spending to GDP is computed as a simple average. Similar results are obtained when using GDP-weighted averages. GDP = gross domestic product; LAC = Latin America and the Caribbean. Refer to Annex 1A for definitions of LAC countries, high-income countries, and low- and middle-income countries without LAC.

cycle and are thus more frequent but much smaller in nature. Moreover, these ratchet effects are partially offset by frequent fiscal adjustments after periods of sustained growth of public debt.

To better see this mechanism in action, figure 1.3 plots the residuals (unexplained variation) in public spending around the Great Recession once we control for economic development, as suggested by Wagner's law, and time-invariant country-specific characteristics, such as differences in institutional quality, size of the economy, economic openness, and demographics, as well as cultural and political backgrounds.[6]

Given their more liberal attitudes toward public spending and their relatively large welfare systems, residuals from OECD economies are positive and consistently higher than the sample average (zero line). During the economic expansion before the Great Recession, there is no increase in public spending beyond the average among these countries. Fiscal efforts associated with countercyclical policies during the Great Recession bumped spending about 5 percentage points of gross domestic product (GDP), and then, as the economy improved, spending went back to a level slightly higher than the precrisis level because of some settling of the fiscal efforts. Importantly, there is no trend in high-income economies over time.

A different story appears to be true for large economies in Latin America and the Caribbean (LAC). For these countries, we observe a tendency to increase public spending significantly during times of economic bonanza and not decrease it during the subsequent periods of economic downturn. This implied downward rigidity in public spending creates an asymmetry in the spending behavior along the business cycle, thus generating spasmodic increases in the public sector over time.

There is, nonetheless, substantial heterogeneity among low- and middle-income economies in how they have increased the size of their governments over time.

FIGURE 1.3: **Augmented Wagner's Law Residuals**

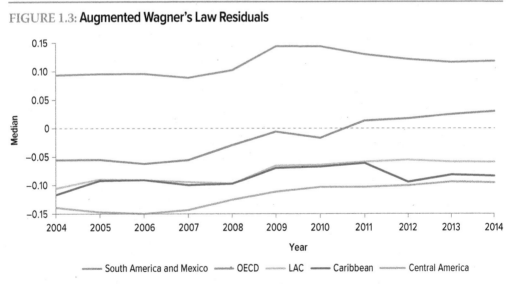

Source: Original calculations based on data from the International Monetary Fund World Economic Outlook database (various years).
Note: LAC = Latin America and the Caribbean; OECD = Organisation for Economic Co-operation and Development.

FIGURE 1.4: Relative Changes in Public Expenditure around Wagner's Law

a. Argentina

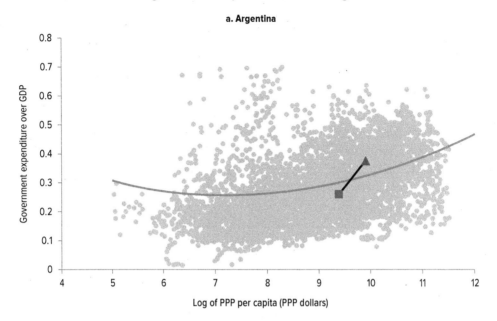

b. Brazil

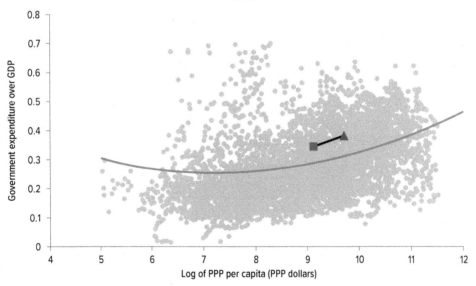

(Continued)

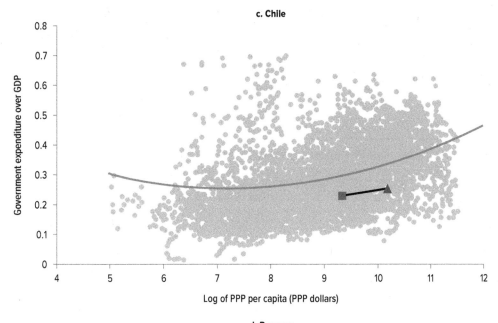

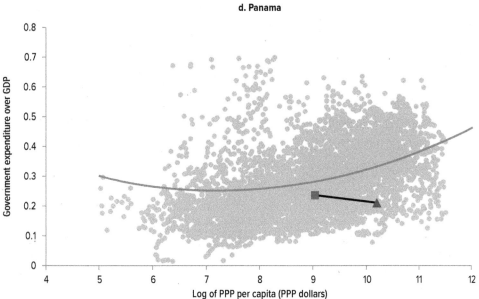

Source: Original calculations based on data from the International Monetary Fund World Economic Outlook database (various years).
Note: Blue dots represent country-year data points. The black line represents a quadratic fit. The starting point (red square) represents the values of the variables in 2000, and the ending point (green triangle) represents the values of the variables for 2019. GDP = gross domestic product; PPP = purchasing power parity.

Figure 1.4 shows that Argentina has experienced a large increase in public spending since 2000, outpacing the country's economic growth. Brazil has also expanded its public sector beyond what its economic development dictated. Panama, at the other extreme, has decreased the share of public spending even as the economy has grown considerably over time. In this particular case, and similar to other small nations in Central America, government officials have displayed a clear aversion to taxation. This conservative view on revenues has constrained the government's ability to spend and hence the size of the public sector over time. Chile is an interesting case because its very moderate increase in the share of public spending since 2000 and the size of its public sector well below what Wagner's law would dictate may be, in part, due to a measurement issue because some typically public spending components such as pensions are operated through a private-public partnership.[7]

Figure 1.5 again uses residuals from Wagner's law around the period of the Great Recession to showcase the heterogeneity in the evolution of public spending across

FIGURE 1.5: **Augmented Wagner's Law Residuals: Large versus Small Latin American Economies**

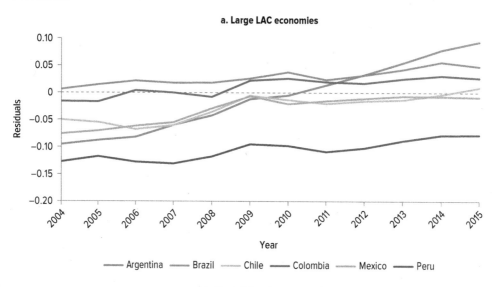

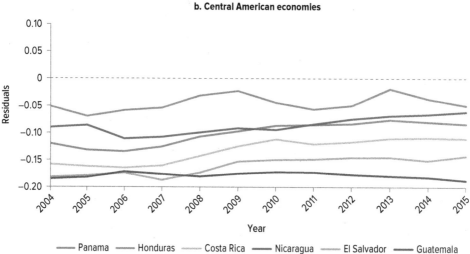

Source: Original calculations for this publication based on data from the International Monetary Fund World Economic Outlook database (various years).
Note: LAC = Latin America and the Caribbean.

LAC countries. Panel a shows how large economies in LAC follow a clear upper trend before and after the recession and stayed flat in 2008 and 2009. Meanwhile, small countries in Central America display barely any change across the entire sample period.

Composition of Public Spending: Going beyond "Big G"

Not only the levels and evolution of overall public spending are different across high- and low- and middle-income economies, but the composition of public spending and the evolution of its individual components also differ greatly among these economies.

A widely used decomposition of primary public spending (total spending excluding interest payments) separates spending elements that are directed by legal mandates (automatic spending) from those that are left to the discretion of the current government (discretionary spending). In automatic spending, we find spending on social transfers and social insurance. Social transfers are divided between social security (mainly covering the elder population with pensions or disability benefits) and family programs. Theoretically, spending on social transfers depends on longer-term structural parameters, such as poverty levels or demographics. However, social insurance led by unemployment benefits is, by construction, countercyclical because spending increases in times of economic recession and high unemployment and decreases as workers find jobs during economic recovery. For discretionary spending, we have public consumption, which covers costs associated with the provision of public goods and services, including government purchase of intermediate goods and services, payment of public wages, and public investment.

Following this decomposition of primary spending, figure 1.6 shows how public expenditure in high-income economies is dominated by automatic spending. Most of it is concentrated around social security, although spending on unemployment insurance grows significantly during recessions. However, low- and middle-income markets tend to spend the most on discretionary spending. Leaning on automatic or discretionary spending leads to differences in cyclicality as well as in the evolution of the relative weights of these components over time.

Looking at social transfers, figure 1.7 shows that pensions have increased significantly in both high-income economies and in our sample of middle-income countries in LAC. Pensions and health expenditure, represented by "social benefits" in figure 1.7, make up the bulk of total expenditure in both sets of countries. Another important feature of LAC shown in figure 1.7 is the lack of effective unemployment insurance, an important automatic stabilizer. As high-income economies enter recessionary periods, such as in 2009, unemployment spending grows (up to 5 percent of total spending), automatically creating a countercyclical effect on income and consumption.

Unfortunately, this mechanism only works among formal workers. The predominance of informality in low- and middle-income markets makes unemployment insurance largely ineffective in these economies.[8] The levels of government consumption,

FIGURE 1.6: Evolution of Components of Government Spending: Spending Decomposition in Low- and Middle-Income versus High-Income Economies

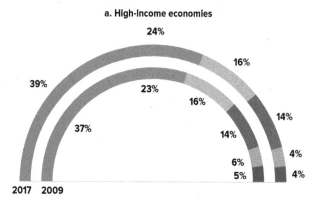

a. High-income economies

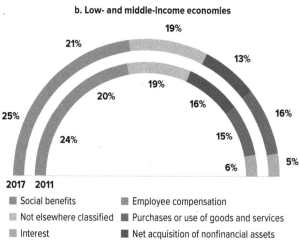

b. Low- and middle-income economies

- Social benefits
- Not elsewhere classified
- Interest
- Employee compensation
- Purchases or use of goods and services
- Net acquisition of nonfinancial assets

Source: Original calculations for this publication based on data from the International Monetary Fund World Economic Outlook database (2019).
Note: High-income economies = Australia, Belgium, Canada, Denmark, France, Germany, Greece, Ireland, Israel, Italy, Luxembourg, Netherlands, Norway, Portugal, Slovak Republic, Slovenia, Spain, Sweden, Switzerland, and United States.
Source: Original calculations for this publication based on data from the International Monetary Fund World Economic Outlook database (2019).
Note: Low- and middle-income economies = Chile; Colombia; Hungary; Korea, Rep.; Peru; Philippines; Poland; Russian Federation; Saudi Arabia; South Africa; Thailand; Türkiye; United Arab Emirates.

which include costs associated with the provision of public goods encompassing education, health, and public safety, are similar across both groups of countries, and the share of public investment is much larger in low- and middle-income markets. It is worth noting that the larger share of public investment is barely enough to bring low- and middle-income economies up to the levels of public capital enjoyed by high-income economies. Moreover, significant changes in the composition of public spending have occurred over time. Spending categories experiencing lesser rigidities and lacking strong constituencies have suffered the lion's share of fiscal adjustments. A relevant example is a steady

FIGURE 1.7: Evolution of Components of Public Social Spending: Transfers in Latin America and the Caribbean versus High-Income Economies

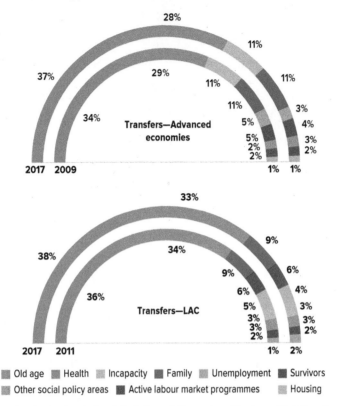

Source: Original calculations based on data from the Organisation for Economic Co-operation and Development Social Expenditure Database and United Nations Economic Commission for Latin America and the Caribbean data.

Note: High-income economies = Australia, Austria, Belgium, Canada, Czechia, Denmark, Estonia, Finland, France, Germany, Greece, Iceland, Ireland, Israel, Italy, Japan, Korea, Rep. of; Latvia, Lithuania, Luxembourg, Netherlands, New Zealand, Norway, Portugal, Slovak Republic, Slovenia, Spain, Sweden, Switzerland, United Kingdom, and United States. LAC = Latin America and the Caribbean. LAC = Argentina, Brazil, Chile, Colombia, Costa Rica, Mexico, and Uruguay

decrease in the share of capital spending on total primary spending since 1990 (refer to figure 1.8). By 2019, the share of public investment relative to that of current spending in low- and middle-income markets had decreased by 9 percentage points. However, the share of public investment in high-income economies has remained remarkably stable, losing around 2 percentage points during this period.

Given the large differences in economic returns (see Auerbach and Gorodnichenko 2012; Ilzetzki, Mendoza, and Végh 2013; Riera-Crichton, Vegh, and Vuletin 2015) and redistributive features (see Goñi, López, and Servén 2011; Lustig 2017) provided by different types of public expenditures, these compositional changes may have long-term detrimental effects on growth and inequality. Thus, a better understanding of procyclicality across the major components of public spending can, for example, lead to the more efficient design of fiscal adjustments (see Easterly and Serven 2003; IMF 2015).

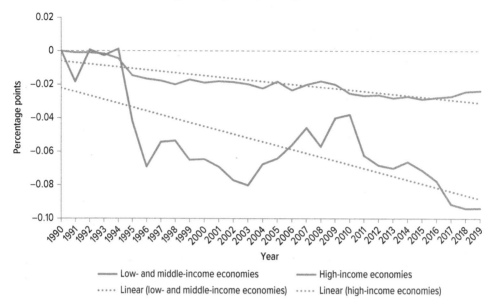

FIGURE 1.8: Evolution of Bias against Capital Spending

Year

— Low- and middle-income economies   — High-income economies
····· Linear (low- and middle-income economies)   ····· Linear (high-income economies)

Source: Original calculations based on data from the International Monetary Fund World Economic Outlook database (2019).
Note: Real government capital spending is defined as general government net acquisition of nonfinancial assets. *Real government total primary spending* is defined as general government total spending net of interest payments. Variables are deflated by the gross domestic product deflator. Bias against capital spending is measured as the difference between the current share of capital spending on total primary spending and that prevailing in 1990.

Efficiency and Effectiveness of Public Spending

The level of spending, however, is not enough—the efficiency with which it is deployed is just as important to achieving desired outcomes. Overall, inefficiencies in spending arise from the relationship among inputs, outputs, and outcomes. Understanding how much a sector or industry can be expected to increase its output through an increase in efficiency, without absorbing further resources (Farrell 1957), should be a key question for policy makers. An array of different objectives in public policy and the fact that public goods are often not sold in open markets create challenges to quantifying the spending inefficiency of the public sector.

Efficiency in public spending is often estimated through the idea of a production possibility frontier where the greater the output for a given input or the lower the input for a given output, the more efficient the activity is. When measuring efficiency, a distinction can be made between technical and allocative efficiency.[9] *Technical efficiency,* on the one hand, is defined as the gains made from moving toward the production possibilities frontier, ensuring that inputs are delivering the maximum outputs. The problem is that technical efficiency does not take into consideration the input costs. *Allocative efficiency,* on the other hand, reflects the link between the optimal combination of inputs taking into account the costs and benefits of the output achieved. In other words, although technical efficiency in the health sector may call for more doctors to deliver better health outputs, the cost of doctors may render this strategy inefficient if there are other spending priorities. *Allocative efficiency* refers to how governments allocate their spending across different functions—education, health, social promotion, investment, defense, generations, levels of government, and so on—to maximize productivity and growth in the economy. To understand allocative efficiency, we would need broad information on the health system, alternatives for inputs, and, most important, costs.

So where are spending inefficiencies coming from? Weak public sector management, negligence, corruption, or a combination thereof inflate the cost of inputs used to produce goods and services. Moreover, spending is inefficiently allocated among government sectors, programs, and populations and over time. Uncovering the roots and measuring the levels of inefficiency in low- and middle-income nations could lead to a large contribution to long-term growth. Beyond taking advantage of additional spending in good times, efficiency gains can also be used to smooth painful adjustments during bad times. Cutting spending across the board, as has been done many times in the past, especially in a recessionary environment, has strong contractionary effects (Riera-Crichton, Vegh, and Vuletin 2015). Utilizing the substantial fiscal space obtained from transforming wasteful and inefficient government spending can also contribute to growth down the road, without adding to inequality.

Looking at the LAC region as a representative of middle-income markets, Izquierdo, Pessino, and Vuletin (2018) provide a measure of the level of public spending inefficiencies on three key components: the cost of goods and services, including capital expenditure; the costs of compensating civil service employees; and part of the cost of subsidies and transfers, which suffer from leakages to those who are not poor. Their analysis is based on technical efficiency, assuming a reasonable allocation of expenditure by function, and, hence, provides estimates of the direct waste of resources reflecting overcost or overuse of inputs for a given outcome.

Figure 1.9 shows that in 2015 the estimated inefficiencies in procurement, civil service, and targeted transfers represented an average amount of waste in the LAC region of 4.4 percent of GDP, larger than the concurrent average spending in health (4.1 percent) and almost as large as the average spending in education (4.8 percent), and these inefficiencies accounted for about 16 percent of average government spending. Estimates range from a low of 1.8 percent of GDP in Chile to 7.2 percent of GDP in Argentina.

Public procurement, including the purchase of goods and services and capital equipment, such as buying computers for primary schools or building a highway or an airport, represents, on average, about 30 percent of total spending in LAC countries (Pessino et al. 2018). As discussed in Izquierdo, Pessino, and Vuletin (2018), public procurement is a magnet for various inefficiency risks originating in waste, mismanagement, and corruption. The waste originating in bribes and padded budgets appears to be enormous: about 26 percent over the cost of projects. The World Bank undertakes reviews of procurement practices and simulations of possible savings. For three countries in LAC, savings of 16–22 percent were estimated on purchases with straightforward modifications of practices and without changing existing procurement laws. For example, in one country savings of 7 percent of purchases were estimated purely from consolidating purchases across

FIGURE 1.9: LAC: Large Waste and Inefficiency Relative to Total Public Expenditure

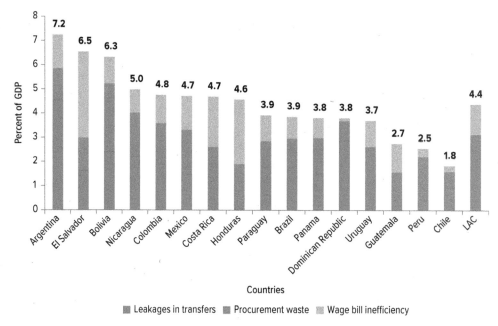

Source: Izquierdo, Pessino, and Vuletin 2018.
Note: LAC = Latin America and the Caribbean; GDP = gross domestic product.

government (bulk buying); 2.5 percent, from the use of electronic catalogs, better use of reverse auctions, and avoiding noncompetitive contracts; 1.3 percent, from more timely processing of contracts; and 1.0 percent, from avoiding seasonal bunching of procurement. Indirectly, eliminating barriers to bidding on government contracts and hence increasing the number of bidders was estimated to generate potential savings of 2.4 percent, and developing special procedures for especially concentrated markets was estimated to generate another 1.8 percent (see World Bank 2021).

On average, in LAC, the wage bill consumes 29 percent of general government spending, and public employees represent about 13 percent of the labor force. The average wage premium in LAC is about 34 percent in favor of public sector employees (Cerda and Pessino 2018) and is one of the highest in the world (IMF 2016). Measures of wage bill inefficiency identify that part of this wage bill premium is driven not by skills but rather mainly by higher union density in the public sector and political economy considerations. According to Izquierdo, Pessino, and Vuletin (2018), the overall wage bill inefficiency in LAC is on average 1.2 percent of GDP (14 percent of wage spending).

On average, about 30 percent of public spending in LAC is on social transfers, including social programs, firm subsidies, and contributory pensions. Transfers targeting errors or leakages—defined as the fraction of program funds that do not reach the intended beneficiaries, typically those who are poor—are at the core of transfers' economic inefficiencies. As shown in figure 1.10, main inefficiencies in transfers, including

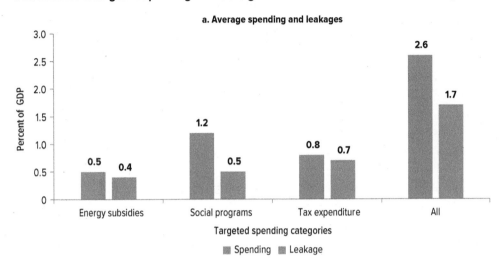

a. Average spending and leakages

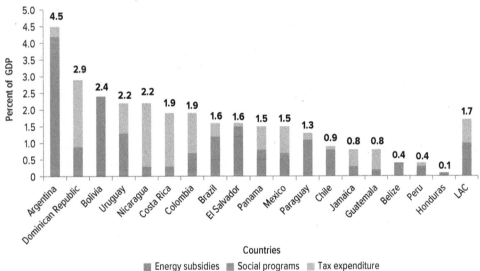

b. Leakages in target expenditures

Source: FIEL 2015, 2017 and Izquierdo, Loo-Kung, and Navajas 2013.
Note: Leakages in average spending refers to waste due to technical or institutional inefficiencies. Leakages in target expenditures are defined as the fraction of program funds that do not reach the intended beneficiaries. GDP = gross domestic product; LAC = Latin America and the Caribbean.

energy subsidies, cash transfers, noncontributory pensions, and tax expenditures to those who are not poor, represent about 1.7 percent of GDP in LAC.

Although the focus in this section so far has been on public spending efficiency, it is worth distinguishing between the concepts of efficiency and effectiveness of public performance. The effectiveness of public spending links inputs or outputs to outcomes (policy objectives). Improvements in welfare or long-term output growth objectives typically serve as outcomes. These outcomes are, of course, affected by a good number of exogenous factors. Thus, effectiveness is more difficult to assess than efficiency. Although it is important to distinguish between output and outcome, the terms are often used interchangeably, and the lines between the two definitions are blurred. A typical example of this problem arises from education spending. Although attainment rates are used in evaluating the output associated with public spending on education, what matters for the outcome target, say economic growth, is the increase in productivity that education and training bring to the overall working-age population. The effectiveness shows the success of the resources used in achieving the objectives set.

To showcase the lack of effectiveness in public spending in low- and middle-income countries, we turn to two key pillars of productivity for low- and middle-income economies: health and education.

The OECD (2020) *Health at a Glance* report and World Bank (2020) show that health spending in LAC was about US$1,000 per person in 2017, only a quarter of what was spent in OECD countries (adjusted for purchasing power). Government spending and compulsory health insurance represent an average of 54.3 percent of total health spending in LAC, significantly lower than the 73.6 percent in OECD countries. These data show that health systems in the LAC region are heavily dependent on out-of-pocket expenditures or supplemental private insurance from households. Additionally, poor allocation of health spending is slowing down, if not halting, the path toward universal health coverage in low- and middle-income regions such as LAC. OECD (2020) and World Bank (2020) suggest several opportunities where immediate action on the appropriate policies can represent quick fiscal wins from the health sector.

On the education side, a sector already plagued by inefficiencies in low- and middle-income nations, COVID-19 added to the pain by effectively shutting down the education system. Indeed, employers in low- and middle-income countries struggle to find the qualified human capital essential to improve productivity and generate economic growth. Almost 30 percent of employers in LAC, relative to 20 percent of employers in the world, report that an inadequately educated workforce is a major constraint to their current operations, the highest of all regions. As important, it has also long been established that education offers the most effective path to upward mobility and lower inequality but that uneven access and quality of educational services present a barrier to forming more equitable societies.

As figure 1.11 shows, learning outcomes in LAC are clearly lagging. The 15-year-olds in the region were already three years behind their OECD comparators in reading, mathematics, and science—and this was before COVID-19 hit.

Beyond the overall lag in educational outcomes relative to developed nations, as figure 1.12 shows, LAC is also plagued by large inequalities in the distribution of educational attainment. During the pandemic, remote learning was the most commonly used strategy to compensate for school closures, but most lower socioeconomic status families lack access to the internet at modest costs, and hence students could not get access to online education platforms and download homework assignments on smartphones, flip phones, or tablets. This implies that losses from COVID-19 will further exacerbate

FIGURE 1.11: Comparison of PISA Reading, Mathematics, and Science Scores for Students in Latin America and the Caribbean and in Organisation for Economic Co-operation and Development Countries

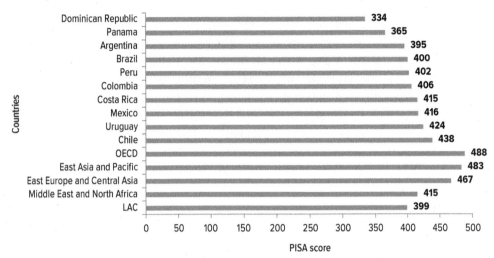

Source: World Bank 2021.
Note: For PISA scores, 40 points = one grade level. OECD = Organisation for Economic Co-operation and Development; PISA = Programme for International Student Assessment.

FIGURE 1.12: Regressive Patterns in Education Quality

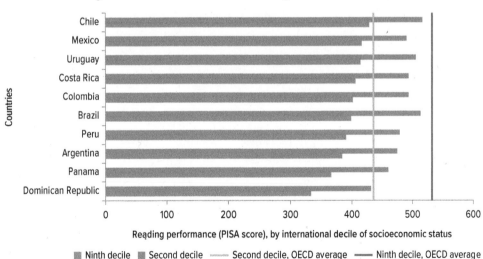

Source: Original calculations based on OECD 2022 and World Bank 2021.
Note: For PISA scores, 40 points = one grade level. OECD = Organisation for Economic Co-operation and Development; PISA = Programme for International Student Assessment.

what figure 1.12 shows to be an already highly unequal distribution of educational attainment. Students in many countries in the bottom quintile are lagging at least two years behind their counterparts in the top quintile.

Some may argue that the low outcomes in education showcased in figure 1.12 may be the result of scarce spending, and, thus, the outcomes obtained, although ineffective, may still be considered efficient. Frontier analysis brings both dimensions together, plotting a measure of the size of inputs compared with the resulting outcomes. Countries delivering the maximum outcomes given their input investment mark the efficiency frontier.

Continuing with our education theme, figure 1.13 plots public spending on education against two learning scores.

Low- and middle-income economies nations tend to spend amounts similar to many high-income economies but are rewarded with lower enrollment rates. A similar story ensues with PISA scores. Increasing the effectiveness of education spending in the low- and middle-income world could lead to large increases in human capital and overall economic productivity without having to increase public spending.

To sum up, in this chapter we have shown that the evolution, composition, and efficiency of public spending differs greatly between high-income economies and low- and middle-income markets. In normal times, high-income economies increase the size of the public sector smoothly as their economies grow. Large shocks such as the two world wars create large discrete jumps in the size of the public sector among these economies. Relatively insulated from these large shocks, low- and middle-income markets tend to undergo smaller ratcheted surges in their public spending after cyclical expansions of their economies.

FIGURE 1.13: **Frontier Analysis of Secondary Education Efficiency**

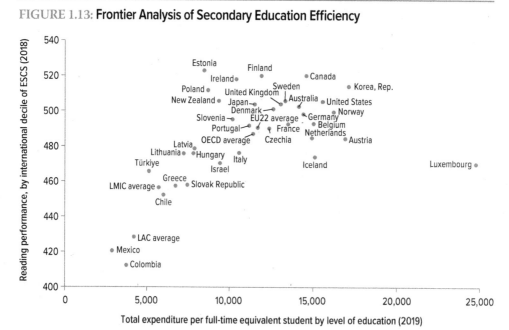

Source: Original calculations based on OECD 2022 and World Bank 2021.
Note: ESCS = economic, social, and cultural status; LAC = Latin America and the Caribbean; LMIC = low- and middle-income country; OECD = Organisation for Economic Co-operation and Development.

In terms of composition of spending, high-income economies spend heavily on automatic spending such as social benefits and unemployment insurance. low- and middle-income markets, however, tend to spend largely on discretionary spending such as public consumption, salaries, and investment. In these countries, the lack of effective unemployment insurance schemes is compensated by family programs and other conditional cash transfers. Although spending on social benefits and especially on pensions has been expanding in both sets of countries, low- and middle-income markets have been slowly but decisively moving away from public investment toward public consumption.

Finally, compared with high-income economies, low- and middle-income markets spend inefficiently and ineffectively. A recent study by Izquierdo, Pessino, and Vuletin (2018) shows overall leakages in public spending worth 4.4 percent of total GDP in Latin America. On the one hand, correcting for these inefficiencies could cover most public deficits in the region. On the other hand, increasing effectiveness of public spending, especially in areas such as health, education, and public safety, could help escape the low productivity trap and accelerate economic growth in the near future.

Annex 1A: Categorization of Countries

TABLE 1A.1: **Categorization of Countries in Chapter 1 Figures**

Figure	Category	Countries Included
Figure 1.1	Low- and middle-income LAC	Argentina, Bolivia, Brazil, Chile, Colombia, Costa Rica, Ecuador, Jamaica, Mexico, and Peru
	Low- and middle-income East Asia	Malaysia, Philippines, Thailand, and Viet Nam
	High-income economies	Australia; Austria; Belgium; Canada; Denmark; Finland; France; Germany; Hong Kong SAR, China; Ireland; Israel; Italy; Japan; Korea, Rep. Netherlands; New Zealand; Norway; Portugal; Spain; Sweden; Switzerland; United Kingdom; and United States
	Other countries included	Afghanistan; Albania; Algeria; Angola; Antigua and Barbuda; Armenia; Aruba; Azerbaijan; Bahamas, The; Bahrain; Bangladesh; Barbados; Belarus; Belize; Benin; Bhutan; Bosnia and Herzegovina; Botswana; Brunei Darussalam; Bulgaria; Burkina Faso; Burundi; Cabo Verde; Cambodia; Cameroon; Central African Republic; Chad; China; Comoros; Congo, Dem. Rep.; Congo, Rep.; Côte d'Ivoire; Croatia; Cyprus; Czechia Djibouti; Dominica; Dominican Republic; Egypt, Arab Rep.; El Salvador; Equatorial Guinea; Eritrea; Estonia; Eswatini; Ethiopia; Fiji; Gabon; Gambia, The; Georgia; Ghana; Greece; Grenada; Guatemala; Guinea; Guinea-Bissau; Guyana; Haiti; Honduras; Hungary; Iceland; India; Indonesia; Iran, Islamic Rep.; Iraq; Jordan; Kazakhstan; Kenya; Kosovo; Kuwait; Kyrgyz Republic; Lao PDR; Latvia; Lebanon; Lesotho; Liberia; Lithuania; Madagascar; Malawi; Maldives; Mali; Malta; Marshall Islands; Mauritania; Mauritius; Micronesia, Fed. Sts.; Moldova; Mongolia; Montenegro; Morocco; Mozambique; Myanmar; Namibia; Nepal; Netherlands; New Zealand; Nicaragua; Niger; Nigeria; North Macedonia; Oman; Pakistan; Panama; Papua New Guinea; Paraguay; Peru; Poland; Puerto Rico; Romania; Russian Federation; Rwanda; San Marino; São Tomé and Príncipe; Saudi Arabia; Senegal; Serbia; Seychelles; Sierra Leone; Slovak Republic; Slovenia; Solomon Islands; South Africa; South Sudan; Sri Lanka; St. Kitts and Nevis; St. Lucia; St. Vincent and the Grenadines; Sudan; Suriname; Tajikistan; Tanzania; Timor-Leste; Togo; Tonga; Trinidad and Tobago; Tunisia; Türkiye; Uganda; Ukraine; United Arab Emirates; Uruguay; Uzbekistan; Vanuatu; Venezuela, RB; Yemen, Rep.; Zambia; Zimbabwe

(continued)

TABLE 1A.1: **Categorization of Countries in Chapter 1 Figures (continued)**

Figure	Category	Countries Included
Figure 1.2	LAC countries	Antigua and Barbuda; Argentina; Bahamas, The; Barbados; Belize; Bolivia; Brazil; Chile; Colombia; Costa Rica; Cuba; Dominica; Dominican Republic; Ecuador; El Salvador; Grenada; Guatemala; Guyana; Haiti; Honduras; Jamaica; Mexico; Nicaragua; Panama; Paraguay; Peru; St. Kitts and Nevis; St. Lucia; St. Vincent and the Grenadines; Suriname; Trinidad and Tobago; Uruguay; Venezuela, RB
	High-income countries	Australia; Austria; Belgium; Canada; Denmark; Finland; France; Germany; Greece; Iceland; Ireland; Italy; Japan; Korea, Rep.; Luxembourg; Netherlands; New Zealand; Norway; Portugal; Spain; Sweden; Switzerland; United Kingdom; United States
	Low- and middle income countries without LAC	Afghanistan; Albania; Algeria; Angola; Armenia; Azerbaijan; Bahrain; Bangladesh; Belarus; Benin; Bhutan; Bosnia and Herzegovina; Botswana; Brunei Darussalam; Bulgaria; Burkina Faso; Burundi; Cabo Verde; Cambodia; Cameroon; Central African Republic; Chad; China; Comoros; Congo, Dem. Rep.; Congo, Rep.; Côte d'Ivoire; Croatia; Cyprus; Czechia; Djibouti; Egypt, Arab. Rep.; Equatorial Guinea; Eritrea; Estonia; Eswatini; Ethiopia; Federal Republic of Germany; Fiji; Gabon; Gambia, the; Georgia; German Democratic Republic; Ghana; Guinea; Guinea-Bissau; Hong Kong SAR, China; Hungary; India; Indonesia; Iran, Islamic Rep.; Iraq; Israel; Jordan; Kazakhstan; Kenya; Kiribati; Korea, Dem. Peoples Rep.; Kuwait; Kyrgyz Republic; Lao PDR; Latvia; Lebanon; Lesotho; Liberia; Libya; Lithuania; Madagascar; Malawi; Malaysia; Maldives; Mali; Malta; Marshall Islands; Mauritania; Mauritius; Micronesia, Fed. Sts.; Moldova; Mongolia; Montenegro; Morocco; Mozambique; Myanmar; Namibia; Nauru; Nepal; Niger; Nigeria; North Macedonia; Oman; Pakistan; Palau; Papua New Guinea; Philippines; Poland; Qatar; Romania; Russian Federation; Rwanda; Samoa; Saudi Arabia; Senegal; Serbia; Serbia and Montenegro; Seychelles; Sierra Leone; Singapore; Slovak Republic; Slovenia; Solomon Islands; Somalia; South Africa; South Sudan; Sri Lanka; Sudan; Syrian Arab Republic; São Tomé and Príncipe; Taiwan; Tajikistan; Tanzania; Thailand; Timor-Leste; Togo; Tonga; Tunisia; Turkmenistan; Tuvalu; Türkiye; Uganda; Ukraine; United Arab Emirates; USSR; Uzbekistan; Vanuatu; Viet Nam; Yemen, Rep.; Yugoslavia; Zambia; Zimbabwe
Figure 1.8	High-income economies	Belgium, Canada, Denmark, Finland, Ireland, Italy, Japan, Norway, Switzerland, and United Kingdom
	Low- and middle-income economies	Algeria; Bahamas, The; Bahrain; Bangladesh; Benin; Botswana; Brunei Darussalam; Burkina Faso; Central African Republic; Chile; Comoros; Congo, Rep. Costa Rica; Djibouti; Dominica; Equatorial Guinea; Ethiopia; Gabon; Ghana; Guinea; Honduras; Iceland; Jamaica; Jordan; Kuwait; Lesotho; Libya; Madagascar; Malaysia; Maldives; Mexico; Morocco; Mozambique; Oman; Paraguay; Philippines; Saudi Arabia; Seychelles; St. Lucia; St. Vincent and Grenadines; Sudan; Suriname; Swaziland; Togo; Trinidad and Tobago; and Yemen, Rep.

Note: LAC = Latin America and the Caribbean.

Notes

1. See Karras (1994), Mamatzakis (2001), Voss (2002), Narayan (2004), and Cavallo and Daude (2011) for empirical findings showing public investment crowding out private investment.

2. Relative exposure may depend on the portfolio of countries that act as trade partners. Rodrik (1998) also shows that countries exposed to large terms of trade volatility tend to have larger governments.

3. As an alternative view, a good number of papers, such as Solow (1956), Baumol and Bowen (1965), Pigou (1928), and Dalton (1965), approached the determination of government expenditure as another piece in the puzzle of social welfare maximization.

4. It is worth noting that the low- and middle-income economies' average hides a fair amount of heterogeneity across regions. Although Latin America and the Caribbean and Africa have increased their public sectors steadily over time, East Asian economies, in general, have kept their government size relative to the size of the economy constant.

5. On the empirical side, these theories were tested in work by Meltzer and Richard (1981), Persson and Tabellini (1990), Barro (1989a, 1989b), Demirbas (1999), Henrekson (1993), Hondroyiannis and Papapetrou (1995), Bohl (1996), Payne and Ewing (1996), Lin (1995), Ram (1986), Beck (1979), Abizadeh and Yousefi (1988), Landau (1983), and Saunders (1988), among others.

6. Residuals are obtained from fitting the following panel data regression:

$$Government\ Expenditure_{it} = \alpha + \mu_i + \beta_1 LogRGDP_{it} + \beta_2 LogRGDP_{it}^2 + \varepsilon_{it},$$

where LogRGDP is the log of real gross domestic product per capita at purchasing power parity prices and μ_i is a set of idiosyncratic country fixed effects. Our sample covers the same sample as figure 1.1. Note that because the median residual should be around zero, not much can be inferred about global trends of government expenditure from this metric. Nonetheless, when dividing our residuals into subsamples, interesting trends emerge.

7. Colombia, Mexico, and Peru also have private, fully funded defined contribution systems competing with public pensions.

8. Poor coverage of unemployment insurance among low- and middle-income markets is further explored in chapter 3.

9. See Schick (1998) for a detailed framework on the basic elements of public expenditure management.

References

Abizadeh, S., and M. Yousefi. 1988. "Growth of Government Expenditure: The Case of Canada." *Public Finance Quarterly* 16 (1): 78–100.

Alesina, A., and R. Wacziarg. 1998. "Openness, Country Size and Government." *Journal of Public Economics* 69 (3): 305–21.

Alvarez, R. M., G. Garrett, and P. Lange. 1991. "Government Partisanship, Labor Organization, and Macroeconomic Performance." *American Political Science Review* 85 (2): 539–56.

Aschauer, D. A. 1989. "Does Public Capital Crowd Out Private Capital?" *Journal of Monetary Economics* 24 (2): 171–88.

Auerbach, A. J., and Y. Gorodnichenko. 2012. "Measuring the Output Responses to Fiscal Policy." *American Economic Journal: Economic Policy* 4 (2): 1–27.

Barro, R. J. 1989a. "A Cross-Country Study of Growth, Saving and Government." Working Paper 2855, National Bureau of Economic Research, Cambridge, MA.

Barro, R. J. 1989b. "Economic Growth in a Cross Section of Countries." Working Paper 3120, National Bureau of Economic Research, Cambridge, MA.

Baumol, W. J., and W. G. Bowen. 1965. "On the Performing Arts: The Anatomy of Their Economic Problems." *American Economic Review* 55 (1/2): 495–502.

Beck, M. 1979. "Public Sector Growth: A Real Perspective." *Public Finance* 34 (3): 313–56.

Bird, R. M., J. Martinez-Vazquez, and B. Torgler. 2014. "Societal Institutions and Tax Effort in Developing Countries." *Annals of Economics and Finance* 15 (1): 185–230.

Blais, A., D. Blake, and S. Dion. 1993. "Do Parties Make a Difference? Parties and the Size of Government in Liberal Democracies." *American Journal of Political Science* 37 (1): 40–62.

Blais, A., D. Blake, and S. Dion. 1996. "Do Parties Make a Difference? A Reappraisal." *American Journal of Political Science* 40 (2): 514–20.

Bohl, M. T. 1996. "Some International Evidence on Wagner's Law." *Public Finance = Finances Publiques* 51 (2): 185–200.

Cavallo, E., and C. Daude. 2011. "Public Investment in Developing Countries: A Blessing or a Curse?" *Journal of Comparative Economics* 39 (1): 65–81.

Cerda, R., and C. Pessino. 2018. *How Large Are Fiscal Wage Gaps in Latin America? How Can They Be Corrected?* Washington, DC: Inter-American Development Bank.

Cusack, T., T. Notermans, and M. Rein. 1989. "Political-Economic Aspects of Public Employment." *European Journal of Political Research* 17 (4): 471–500.

Dalton, G. 1965. "History, Politics, and Economic Development in Liberia." *Journal of Economic History* 25 (4): 569–91.

De Haan, J., and J. E. Sturm. 1994. "Political and Institutional Determinants of Fiscal Policy in the European Community." *Public Choice* 80 (1): 157–72.

De Haan, J., and J. E. Sturm. 1997. "Political and Economic Determinants of OECD Budget Deficits and Government Expenditures: A Reinvestigation." *European Journal of Political Economy* 13 (4): 739–50.

Demirbas, S. 1999. "Cointegration Analysis-Causality Testing and Wagner's Law: The Case of Turkey, 1950–1990." Discussion Papers in Economics 99/3, University of Leicester, Leicester, United Kingdom.

Easterly, W., and S. Rebelo. 1993. "Fiscal Policy and Economic Growth." *Journal of Monetary Economics* 32 (3): 417–58.

Easterly, W., and L. Serven, eds. 2003. *The Limits of Stabilization: Infrastructure, Public Deficits and Growth in Latin America.* Washington, DC: World Bank; Palo Alto: Stanford University Press.

Erden, L., and R. Holcombe. 2005. "The Effects of Public Investment on Private Investment in Developing Economies." *Public Finance Review* 33 (5): 575–602.

Farrell, M. J. 1957. "The Measurement of Productive Efficiency." *Journal of the Royal Statistical Society: Series A (General)* 120 (3): 253–81.

Fedotenkov, I., and G. Idrisov. 2021. "A Supply-Demand Model of Public Sector Size." *Economic Systems* 45 (2): 100869.

FIEL (Fundación de Investigaciones Económicas Latinoamericanas). 2015. *Mejorando la calidad y la eficiencia del gasto público en energía y asistencia social en América Latina y el Caribe.* Buenos Aires: FIEL.

FIEL (Fundación de Investigaciones Económicas Latinoamericanas). 2017. *Calidad y eficiencia del gasto público en América Latina y el Caribe: actualización de estimaciones de niveles de gasto y filtraciones en asistencia social, energía y gasto tributario.* Buenos Aires: FIEL.

Garrett, G. 1998. *Partisan Politics in the Global Economy.* Cambridge: Cambridge University Press.

Goñi, E., J. H. López, and L. Servén. 2011. "Fiscal Redistribution and Income Inequality in Latin America." *World Development* 39 (9): 1558–69.

Greene, J., and D. Villanueva. 1991. "Private Investment in Developing Countries: An Empirical Analysis." *IMF Staff Papers* 38 (1): 33–58.

Henrekson, M. 1993. "Wagner's Law—A Spurious Relationship?" *Public Finance* 48 (3): 406–15.

Hondroyiannis, G., and E. Papapetrou. 1995. "An Examination of Wagner's Law for Greece: A Cointegration Analysis." *Public Finance = Finances Publiques* 50 (1): 67–79.

Ilzetzki, E., E. G. Mendoza, and C. A. Végh. 2013. "How Big (Small?) Are Fiscal Multipliers?" *Journal of Monetary Economics* 60 (2): 239–54.

IMF (International Monetary Fund). 2015. *Making Public Investment More Efficient.* IMF Staff Report. Washington, DC: IMF.

IMF (International Monetary Fund). 2016. *Managing Government Compensation and Employment—Institutions, Policies, and Reform Challenges.* Washington, DC: IMF.

Iversen, T., and T. R. Cusack. 2000. "The Causes of Welfare State Expansion: Deindustrialization or Globalization?" *World Politics* 52 (3): 313–49.

Izquierdo, A., R. Loo-Kung, and F. Navajas. 2013. *Resistiendo el canto de las sirenas financieras en Centroamérica: una ruta hacia un gasto eficiente con más crecimiento.* Washington, DC: Inter-American Development Bank.

Izquierdo, A., C. Pessino, and G. Vuletin, eds. 2018. *Better Spending for Better Lives: How Latin America and the Caribbean Can Do More with Less.* Washington, DC: Inter-American Development Bank.

Karras, G. 1994. "Government Spending and Private Consumption: Some International Evidence." *Journal of Money, Credit, and Banking* 26 (1): 9–22.

Lamartina, S., and A. Zaghini. 2011. "Increasing Public Expenditure: Wagner's Law in OECD Countries." *German Economic Review* 12 (2): 149–64.

Landau, D. 1983. "Government Expenditure and Economic Growth: A Cross-Country Study." *Southern Economic Journal* 49 (3): 783–92.

Lin, C. 1995. "More Evidence on Wagner's Law for Mexico." *Public Finance = Finances publiques* 50 (2): 267–77.

Lustig, N. 2017. "El impacto del sistema tributario y el gasto social en la distribución del ingreso y la pobreza en América Latina: Argentina, Bolivia, Brasil, Chile, Colombia, Costa Rica, Ecuador, El Salvador, Guatemala, Honduras, México, Nicaragua, Perú, República Dominicana, Uruguay y Venezuela Una aplicación del marco metodológico del proyecto Compromiso con la Equidad (CEQ). *El trimestre económico* 84 (335): 493–568.

Mahdavi, S. 2008. "The Level and Composition of Tax Revenue in Developing Countries: Evidence from Unbalanced Panel Data." *International Review of Economics & Finance* 17 (4): 607–17.

Mamatzakis, E. 2001. "Public Spending and Private Investments: Evidence from Greece." *International Economic Journal* 15 (4): 33–46.

Meltzer, A. H., and S. F. Richard. 1981. "A Rational Theory of the Size of Government." *Journal of Political Economy* 89 (5): 914–27.

Milesi-Ferretti, G. M., R. Perotti, and M. Rostagno. 2002. "Electoral Systems and Public Spending." *Quarterly Journal of Economics* 117 (2): 609–57.

Musgrave, R. A. 1959. "The Theory of Multi-Level Public Finance." *Proceedings of the Annual Conference on Taxation under the Auspices of the National Tax Association* 52: 266–78.

Narayan, P. 2004. "Do Public Investments Crowd Out Private Investments? Fresh Evidence from Fiji." *Journal of Policy Modeling* 26 (6): 747–53.

OECD (Organisation for Economic Co-operation and Development). 2020. *Health at a Glance: Europe 2020—State of Health in the EU Cycle.* Paris: OECD Publishing.

OECD (Organisation for Economic Co-operation and Development). 2022. *PISA 2022 Results (Volume I): The State of Learning and Equity in Education.* Paris: PISA (Program for International Student Assessment), OECD Publishing.

Payne, J. E., and B. T. Ewing. 1996. "International Evidence on Wagner's Hypothesis: A Cointegration Analysis." *Public Finance = Finances Publiques* 51 (2): 258–74.

Peacock, A. T., and J. Wiseman. 1961. "Front Matter, the Growth of Public Expenditure in the United Kingdom." In *The Growth of Public Expenditure in the United Kingdom,* 32. Princeton, NJ: Princeton University Press.

Peacock, A. T., and J. Wiseman. 1979. "Approaches to the Analysis of Government Expenditure Growth." *Public Finance Quarterly* 7 (1): 3–23.

Persson, T., and G. Tabellini. 1990. *Macroeconomic Policy, Credibility, and Politics.* Amsterdam: Harwood Academic.

Persson, T., and G. Tabellini. 1999. "The Size and Scope of Government: Comparative Politics with Rational Politicians." *European Economic Review* 43 (4–6): 699–735.

Pessino, C., I. Badin, J. C. Benítez, D. Dborkin, N. Tolsa, and J. Zentner. 2018. *Trends in Public Spending: Insights from a New Latin American Dataset.* Washington, DC: Inter-American Development Bank.

Pigou, A. C. 1928. "An Analysis of Supply." *Economic Journal* 38 (150): 238–57.

Ram, R. 1986. "Government Size and Economic Growth: A New Framework and Some Evidence from Cross-Section and Time-Series Data." *American Economic Review* 76 (1): 191–203.

Riera-Crichton, D., C. A. Vegh, and G. Vuletin. 2015. "Procyclical and Countercyclical Fiscal Multipliers: Evidence from OECD Countries." *Journal of International Money and Finance* 52: 15–31.

Rodrik, D. 1998. "Why Do More Open Economies Have Bigger Governments?" *Journal of Political Economy* 106 (5): 997–1032.

Roubini, N., and J. Sachs. 1989a. "Government Spending and Budget Deficits in the Industrial Countries." *Economic Policy* 4 (8): 99–132.

Roubini, N., and J. Sachs. 1989b. "Political and Economic Determinants of Budget Deficits in the Industrial Democracies." *European Economic Review* 33 (5): 903–33.

Saunders, P. 1988. "Private Sector Shrinkage and the Growth of Industrialized Economies: Comment." *Public Choice* 58 (3): 277–84.

Schick, A. 1998. *A Contemporary Approach to Public Expenditure Management.* Washington, DC: World Bank. https://documents.worldbank.org/curated/en/739061468323718599 /A-contemporary-approach-to-public-expenditure-management.

Schmidt, V. 2002. "Does Discourse Matter in the Politics of Welfare State Adjustment?" *Comparative Political Studies* 35 (2): 168–93.

Solow, R. M. 1956. "A Contribution to the Theory of Economic Growth." *Quarterly Journal of Economics* 70 (1): 65–94.

Stein, E. H., E. Talvi, and A. Grisanti. 1998. *Arreglos institucionales y desempeño fiscal: La experiencia latinoamericana.* Washington, DC: Inter-American Development Bank, Research Department.

Voss, G. 2002. "Public and Private Investment in the United States and Canada." *Economic Modeling* 19 (4): 641–64.

Wagner, A. 1893. *Grundlegung der politschen Oekonomie.* Leipzig: C. F. Winter.

World Bank. 2020. *The Cost of Staying Healthy.* Latin America and the Caribbean Semiannual Report. Washington, DC: World Bank. https://doi.org/10.1596/978-1-4648-1650-5.

World Bank. 2021. *Recovering Growth: Rebuilding Dynamic Post-COVID-19 Economies amid Fiscal Constraints.* Latin America and the Caribbean Semiannual Report. Washington, DC: World Bank. https://doi.org/10.1596/978-1-4648-1806-6.

2

In "Good Times," a Procyclical, Downwardly Rigid, and Inefficient Public Spending

Introduction

Fiscal anomalies in fiscal policy start in periods of economic bonanza. In good times, economic growth delivers public revenues and relatively low financing costs, alleviating constraints on spending in low- and middle-income markets. Beyond the immediate pros and cons of these procyclical policies—that is, the fact that a larger provision of much-needed public goods could be desirable and heighten economic volatility—low- and middle-income markets tend to increase components of public spending that are difficult to reverse on the opposite side of the cycle (downwardly rigid), such as public wages. Following a cyclical pattern of increases in public consumption leads to steady growth in the size of the public sector, potentially curtailing much-needed fiscal space when bad times finally arrive. In addition, low- and middle-income markets suffer from large inefficiencies in the provision of public goods. Inefficient spending in public education or health leads to low labor productivity and diminishes the future economic returns necessary to repay the original spending. Thus, inefficient and semiprocyclical public consumption in good times sets the stage for fiscal stress even before a recession arrives.

This chapter explores the asymmetric behavior of public consumption throughout the business cycle. We start by reviewing recent findings of overall procyclicality in low- and middle-income markets and its effect on output volatility. We then go beyond "big G" to study the behavior of public consumption—that is, spending dedicated to the provision of public goods—along the business cycle.[1] We finish the chapter by evaluating the costs of the inefficient provision of public goods.

Overall Public Spending Procyclicality in Low- and Middle-Income Markets and Economic Volatility

The public finance literature has pointed to the procyclical fiscal behavior of low- and middle-income markets as the original sin and one of the main culprits of their fiscal woes because it goes against standard Keynesian recipes for moderating the economic cycle. Indeed, recent empirical studies have shown how overall primary spending in low- and middle-income markets is, in general and counterintuitively, positively correlated with the state of the business cycle, rising in good times and decreasing in bad times, even after adjusting for possible reverse causality (Alesina, Campante, and Tabellini 2008; Gavin and Perotti 1997; Ilzetzki and Végh 2008; Jaimovich and Panizza 2007; Kaminsky, Reinhart, and Végh 2004; Mendoza and Oviedo 2006; Rigobon 2004; Talvi and Végh 2005; Tornell and Lane 1999).

Figure 2.1, which updates evidence presented in Kaminsky, Reinhart, and Végh (2004) and later in Frankel, Vegh, and Vuletin (2013), shows the direction and size of the correlation between general government overall primary spending and aggregate output (measured as gross domestic product [GDP]) for 83 countries (20 high-income and 63 low- and middle-income countries) for the period 1980–2019. Dark bars represent high-income economies, and light bars represent low- and middle-income markets. If public spending and GDP tend to move in the same direction (positive correlation), then fiscal policy is said to be procyclical. It follows that countercyclicality is determined by both measures moving in opposite directions (negative correlation). From the figure it is clear that although fiscal policy tends to be mildly countercyclical in high-income economies, it is procyclical in low- and middle-income markets.

This procyclicality has typically been explained through the lens of "inherited initial conditions," such as political distortions and weak institutions (see Talvi and Végh 2005; Tornell and Lane 1999; Velasco 1997), or the lack of financial depth and imperfect access to international credit markets (see Caballero and Krishnamurthy 2004; Gavin et al. 1996; Gavin and Perotti 1997; Riascos and Vegh 2003). It has also been shown that procyclicality of public spending is an important factor explaining the excess economic volatility in low- and middle-income markets.

Frankel, Vegh, and Vuletin (2013) show that institutional frameworks characterized by the protection of property rights, the control of corruption, higher bureaucratic quality, and a strong law-and-order tradition have allowed low- and middle-income countries to "graduate" from procyclicality in the past decade. Using alternative proxies for institutional quality, Céspedes and Velasco (2014) find evidence consistent with Frankel, Vegh, and Vuletin (2013) in a sample of 60 resource-rich countries, and Alesina, Campante, and Tabellini (2008) show that measures of corruption are positively correlated with procyclical fiscal policy.

Low- and middle-income markets indeed suffer from higher economic volatility than their high-income counterparts. To showcase this, and following a large literature, table 2.1 computes the real GDP per capita growth volatility across the main regions of the world. The figures in this table show that, over the past five

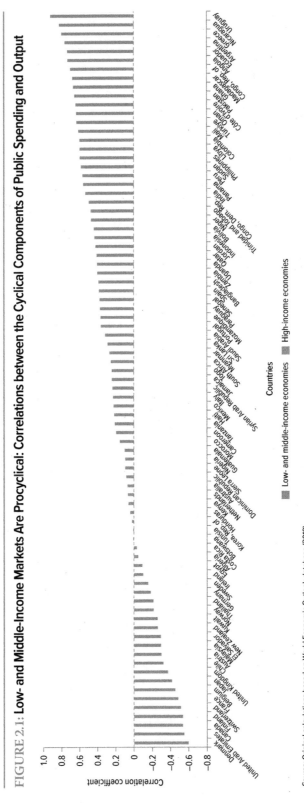

FIGURE 2.1: Low- and Middle-Income Markets Are Procyclical: Correlations between the Cyclical Components of Public Spending and Output

Countries

■ Low- and middle-income economies   ■ High-income economies

Source: Original calculations based on World Economic Outlook database (2019).

Note: The cyclical components have been estimated using the Hodrick-Prescott filter. A positive correlation indicates procyclical fiscal policy; a negative correlation, countercyclical fiscal policy. Real government expenditure is defined as general government overall primary expenditure deflated by the gross domestic product deflator. The panel goes from 1980 to 2019.

TABLE 2.1: Procyclicality Leads to More Volatility, and Low- and Middle-Income Markets Are More Volatile

Variable	High-income economies	LMIC Asia	LMIC Europe	Latin America and the Caribbean	Middle East and North Africa	Sub-Saharan Africa
Output volatility	2.6	4.1	4.6	4.2	7.2	5.2
	(1.0)	(3.3)	(2.5)	(1.2)	(6.1)	(3.4)

Source: Vegh et al. 2018.
Note: Output volatility is measured as the standard deviation of real output growth for each country. Coefficients in the table represent the means of output volatilities for each region. Values in parentheses are the standard deviation of output volatilities in each region. LMIC = low- and middle-income countries.

decades (1970–2017), real GDP per capita growth has ranged from two to almost three times larger in low- and middle-income regions than in their Organisation for Economic Co-operation and Development (OECD) counterparts.

Excess economic volatility causes significant problems for low- and middle-income markets. Through the economic uncertainty that economic volatility creates, it has been linked in the literature to underdeveloped credit markets and the inability of policy makers to effectively protect the country against negative shocks (or take full advantage of positive ones; see, for example, Baez et al. 2017; Loayza and Otker-Robe 2014). Thus, output volatility tends to lower long-run economic performance (see Barrot, Calderón, and Servén 2018; Loayza et al. 2007; Raddatz 2008).

How Does Procyclical Fiscal Policy Contribute to Output Volatility?

A simple Keynesian-based answer would remind us of the direct link between public spending and aggregate demand (through "big G") and how aggregate supply reacts to demand changes in the short run when prices are sticky (that is, when prices are resistant to change, despite shifts in the broad economy suggesting that a different price is optimal). Expanding public spending in good times and contracting it during bad times reinforces the business cycle, creating more output volatility.

Because the direct effect on the aggregate demand of a change in public consumption raises incomes, Keynesian theory predicts additional effects from private consumption and investment that further increase demand and thus output. A large empirical literature has tried to estimate the size of these public spending multipliers. Findings reported in the academic literature vary widely, from negative multipliers to positive ones as high as 4.[2]

A key reason behind such different estimates is that the size of fiscal multipliers depends on various characteristics of the economy in question, including degree of openness, exchange rate regimes, debt level, and monetary stance, among others (see Auerbach and Gorodnichenko 2012, 2013; Huidrom et al. 2020; Ilzetzki, Mendoza, and Végh 2013). The size of the fiscal multipliers also depends on the stage of the business cycle and the type of fiscal policy that is applied (see Bachmann and Sims 2012; Candelon and Lieb 2013; Owyang, Ramey, and Zubairy 2013). The literature has traditionally focused on the size of the multipliers along the business cycle, implicitly assuming that fiscal policy is countercyclical (that is, government spending increases in bad times and falls in good times), as has traditionally been the case (at least on average) for high-income countries. Nonetheless, as shown in Riera-Crichton, Vegh, and Vuletin (2015), this assumption does not hold for low- and middle-income markets, which spend, on average, 64 percent of their time conducting procyclical fiscal policies. Using a global sample of 52 countries (21 high income and 31 low income) for the period 1971–2011, these authors find that distinguishing between procyclical and countercyclical policies is important for the estimation of spending multipliers in low- and middle-income countries because findings show that ignoring whether government spending is going up or down can bias the estimations. Following a simple theoretical example of a full employment (i.e., good times) case with sticky prices, Riera-Crichton, Vegh, and Vuletin find that a decrease in government spending does not affect output (that is, a zero multiplier, at least in the short run) as the private sector rushes in to fill the gap. Meanwhile, an increase in government spending leads, temporally, to a small (around 0.4 after one year) but positive multiplier. On the other side of the cycle (that is, bad times), large multipliers (close to 1.0 after one year) are obtained when government spending decreases, which implies that the traditionally procyclical fiscal policy followed by low- and middle-income countries amplifies the business cycle but mostly during downturns (part of the so-called "when-it-rains-it-pours" phenomenon reported in Kaminsky, Reinhart, and Végh 2004).

How much of this additional volatility is induced by fiscal policy? To capture the full impact of fiscal procyclicality on any given economy, we must consider the fact that a fiscal shock can have a direct and contemporaneous impact on output growth, but it can also lead to lagged indirect effects through changes in other important variables in the economy.

Moreover, changes in some variables may be persistent over time, leading to dynamic effects on output growth and other variables. To account for all these potentially important mechanisms, we estimate a structural vector autoregression (SVAR) model for each country with available data. The SVAR model allows us to combine exposure (that is, underlying shock volatility) with vulnerability (that is, the estimated coefficients in each regression) to compute a variance decomposition of the dependent variable. The variance decomposition (also known as forecast error variance decomposition) helps us identify the amount of information that each variable contributes to the other variables in the system. In other words, it measures the share of the forecast error variance of each of the variables explained by exogenous shocks to the other variables.

Table 2.2 displays the medians of the real output growth variance decompositions across different regions after two years of the original shock. In line with recent papers, we find that external factors explain a large share of the forecast error variance in all regions, with commodity terms of trade being a very important source of volatility for all regions. Nonetheless, internal demand also explains a relatively large share of output volatility, and public spending seems to be its most significant component. Overall,

TABLE 2.2: Variance Decomposition of GDP Growth Volatility

Percent of total variance of GDP growth after two years

Region	All Countries	High-Income Economies	LMIC Asia	LMIC Europe	Latin America and the Caribbean
External factors	**24.0**	**27.9**	**16.8**	**23.1**	**20.3**
Commodities TOT growth	10.5	10.7	8.5	10.1	11.2
	(8.7)	(10.6)	(12.0)	(4.0)	(5.6)
Real interest rate (United States)	5.2	9.7	6.3	8.7	4.6
	(10.7)	(14.9)	(5.6)	(4.4)	(5.0)
Output growth (United States)	8.3	9.7	6.3	8.7	4.6
	(10.7)	(14.9)	(5.6)	(4.4)	(5.0)
Domestic factors	**14.1**	**13.1**	**16.2**	**18.7**	**14.5**
Real government consumption growth	4.7	4.2	2.6	7.6	6.2
	(11.2)	(4.6)	(4.0)	(5.1)	(23.7)
Trade balance or GDP growth	3.0	3.0	3.0	3.4	2.5
	(4.9)	(4.1)	(2.1)	(5.7)	(5.4)
Domestic real interest rate	4.4	3.9	5.1	6.5	4.1
	(6.0)	(5.5)	(8.1)	(7.9)	(3.4)
Real effective exchange rate growth	2.0	2.0	5.5	1.2	1.7
	(3.0)	(2.3)	(3.6)	(3.8)	(3.6)
Persistence	**50.4**	**45.4**	**57.6**	**53.8**	**55.5**
	(20.3)	(20.2)	(22.7)	(18.6)	(20.7)

Source: Vegh et al. 2018.

Note: The analysis uses a total of 52 economies and covers the period 1960–2017. Bold denotes aggregates. Results are calculated for each individual country. The coefficients in the table represent the means for the countries in each region. Values in parentheses are the standard deviations for each region. GDP = gross domestic product; LMIC = low- and middle-income countries; TOT = terms of trade.

changes in public spending explain about 5 percent of all the variance in output growth. This number may seem small, but it is important to note that output growth is highly persistent. Persistence, measured as past values, explains anywhere between 45 and 55 percent of the total variance of output growth. That means that in Latin America and the Caribbean, for example, only 44 percent of the variance is due to contemporaneous shocks. Of this remaining 44 percent, 6 percent (about one-sixth of the remaining variance) come from changes in public spending.

Procyclicality of Public Consumption Meets Spending Rigidities

Beyond the issues related to heightened economic volatility discussed earlier, cutting back advances in the provision of public goods is difficult and, in many cases, not desirable from a policy standpoint, as is the case in any economy. In other words, a government will have difficulty cutting education or health services during a downturn when these public goods are most desperately needed. This means that a large share of the cyclical increases in public consumption achieved during good times is typically downwardly rigid. Low- and middle-income markets may suffer an even larger challenge when cutting public consumption because most of the expansion is achieved through increases in public wages with their own structural rigidities.

We usually think of public spending rigidities as limits to modifying the level or structure of expenditure over a period imposed by institutional decrees (see Cetrángolo, Jiménez, and Ruiz del Castillo 2010; Echeverry, Bonilla, and Moya 2006; Herrera and Olaberría 2020), although we often see textbook examples contrasting discretionary public spending with rigid categories of spending, such as entitlements, automatic stabilizers, or interest payments on public debt. In fact, discretionary spending may also suffer from serious forms of rigidities. Beyond contractual obligations to pay interests on public debt and public wages and legal mandates protecting entitlements, social contracts, and other public expenditures, institutional weaknesses and political economy arguments may compromise the ability or willingness of governments to apply discretionary cuts to public consumption and the provision of public goods such as education, health, or public safety.

The downward rigidity of public consumption means that low- and middle-income markets are not procyclical but semiprocyclical; in other words, spending increases in good times while remaining relatively constant during recessions. Apart from subjecting the structural size of the public sector to cyclical fluctuations, the procyclical behavior of low- and middle-income markets in good times prevents these economies from self-insuring against a lack of fiscal space during bad times. This behavior is especially costly for economies that traditionally face large tax base volatility and lack of access to international credit during recessions (Gavin et al. 1996; Riascos and Vegh 2003; Talvi and Végh 2005).

So why do these countries overspend in good times? As explained earlier, political economy arguments based on institutional weaknesses may help answer this question. In an early take on the issue, Tornell and Lane (1999) developed a model in which a number of political groups compete for fiscal resources. Using the well-known consequences of the problem of the common pool (Ostrom 1990), they show how this competition leads to a "voracity effect," defined as a disproportionate response of public spending to exogenous shocks in the economy, such as unexpected windfalls from commodity exports. Similarly, Talvi and Végh (2005) proposed a model in which pressures to increase public spending by political actors grow during periods of economic bonanza. Building on the ideas from Tornell and Lane (1999), the literature warns us that the voracity effect and thus the procyclical tendencies of low- and middle-income countries may grow with the number of political actors with distinct goals and constituencies (Lane 2003). Divergent political views and policy objectives among political groups may lead to attempts to exhaust resources while in power and thus may also lead to overspending during good times (Humphreys and Sandbu 2007; Ilzetzki 2011).

Contrary to the overall cyclicality of public spending, the asymmetrical public spending responses to the economic cycle have not been extensively explored in the literature. Among the few studies exploring these issues, Balassone and Francese (2004) find evidence in OECD countries of significant asymmetry in the reaction of fiscal policy to positive and negative cyclical conditions, with budgetary balances deteriorating in contractions and not improving in expansions. This asymmetry appears to have contributed significantly to debt accumulation. Similarly, Hercowitz and Strawczynski (2004) find that the prolonged rise in the spending-to-output ratio is partially explained by cyclical upward ratcheting due to asymmetric fiscal behavior. These authors also analyzed cyclical changes in the composition of government spending (government consumption, transfers and subsidies, and capital expenditure), as well as a possible link between cyclical ratcheting and government weakness. For low- and middle-income countries, Carneiro and Garrido (2015) investigate the extent to which countries behave procyclically or countercyclically in different phases of the business cycle and find a causal link running from stronger institutions to less procyclical fiscal policy, even after controlling for the endogeneity of institutions and other determinants of fiscal policy. Balassone and Kumar (2007) find evidence of exuberance in government expenditures during the boom phase of an economic cycle. They conclude that procyclicality may reflect an inaccurate assessment of the cycle, particularly in low- and middle-income markets during downturns.

Ardanaz and Izquierdo (2017) show how public consumption tends to be significantly procyclical among low- and middle-income countries during good times. Public consumption is by and large made up of the cost of public employment, which can be divided into public wages and salaries and the number of public employees and the purchase of goods and services by the public sector. These are the key expenditures behind the provision of public goods such as education, health, police, and defense. It is not obvious why governments would change, for example, the number of teachers, doctors, police, or military personnel over the business cycle. In principle, such decisions should be related to social preferences and the specific properties of public goods production. Again, political economy arguments may help explain why some expenditures react more heavily to the business cycle than others.

Beyond showing strong procyclicality in good times, empirical evidence points to another important issue with public consumption spending along the business cycle: current spending is clearly downwardly rigid. In other words, although spending seems to increase in good times, it does not seem to decrease in bad ones.

Figure 2.2 compares the growth rates of public spending on salaries and goods and services along the business cycle. Following the downwardly rigid behavior described earlier, emerging markets seem to increase spending at a fast rate during expansions while, on average, not cutting back during recessions. High-income economies, however, seem

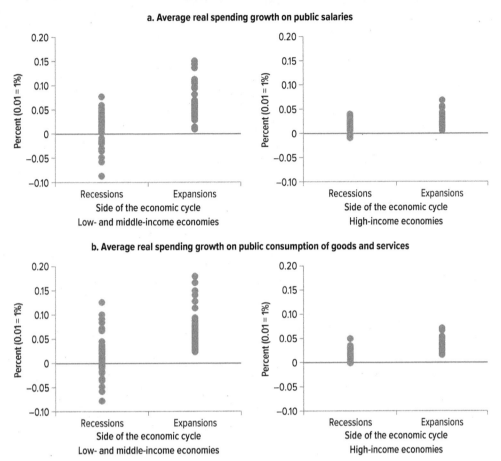

FIGURE 2.2: Average Growth in the Main Components of Primary Government Consumption over the Business Cycle

a. Average real spending growth on public salaries

Low- and middle-income economies

High-income economies

b. Average real spending growth on public consumption of goods and services

Low- and middle-income economies

High-income economies

Source: Original calculations using World Economic Outlook data (1980–2019; not all years are available for all countries).
Note: Mean growth covers all existing observations between 1980 and 2019. Refer to Annex 2A for definitions of low- and middle-income economies and high-income economies.

to slowly increase spending in these categories regardless of the state of the business cycle, thus behaving acyclically.

Similarly, a nonlinear panel regression analysis also shows asymmetric behavior of public consumption between good and bad times in low- and middle-income markets. Figure 2.3 plots the output elasticities of public salaries and public purchases of goods and services at different stages of the business cycle for representative groups of high-income economies and low- and middle-income markets. Because the causal relationship between output and public spending can clearly go both ways, the estimated elasticities are based on an instrumental variable approach in which plausible exogenous income shocks such as terms of trade or foreign demand are used as instruments.[3]

FIGURE 2.3: Output Elasticities of Public Consumption Expenditures over the Business Cycle

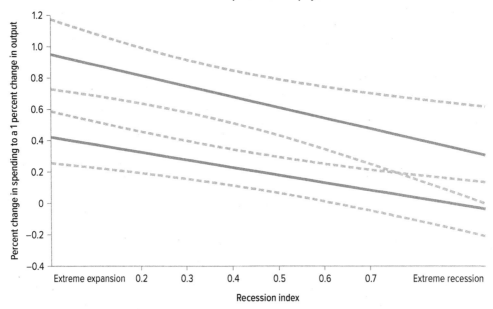

a. Compensation of employees

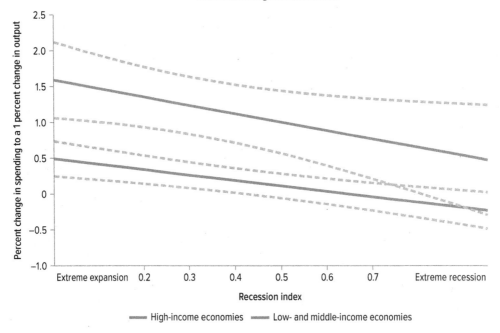

b. Purchases of goods and services

━━━━━ High-income economies ━━━━━ Low- and middle-income economies

Source: Original calculations using World Economic Outlook data (1980–2019; not all years are available for all countries).
Note: The area between the dashed lines represents the 95 percent confidence interval. See Annex 2A for definitions of low- and middle-income economies and high-income economies.

In figures 2.3a and 2.3b, a flat line represents a symmetric behavior of public spending over the business cycle, either procyclical if above zero or countercyclical otherwise. In both figures, high-income economies tend to spend moderately in good times with a statistically insignificant retrenchment in bad times. Spending decisions in low- and middle-income markets, however, tend to be significantly more affected by short-run economic conditions. In these countries, increases in real output during good times would lead to large increases in public consumption. Meanwhile, decreases in output during bad times would lead to much lesser decreases in spending, indicating some sort of spending downward rigidity, and thus to the semiprocyclicality of public consumption.

One of the main problems with the procyclicality of public employment during good times is the fact that, traditionally, public employment spending is downwardly rigid. Although public salaries and employment may increase along with their private counterparts in good times (even at a faster pace, depending on the political distortions afflicting the public sector), they become more rigid during bad times. Downward spending rigidities in public employment are common across high-income and low- and middle-income economies, but whereas the former tend to increase spending along their long-run path of economic development, the latter tend to overspend in good times, diminishing the fiscal space in advance of economic recession.

Macroeconomic textbooks teach us that salaries and wages are, by nature, quite rigid in any market. That may not necessarily translate into labor market rigidity if labor markets are allowed to adjust through the level of employment. Although this is generally the case for private markets in high-income economies, the political economy distortions described here make public employment in low- and middle-income markets extremely rigid during downturns. Moreover, low- and middle-income markets may actively use public employment as a policy tool to provide insurance against exposure to external, undiversifiable risk (Rodrik 2000) or as a tool to redistribute rents or compensate for inequality or social fragmentation (Alesina, Baqir, and Easterly 2000).

Procyclicality in public consumption during business cycle expansions and downward rigidity during contractions start to pave the road to fiscal unsustainability issues for low- and middle-income markets.

In Good Times, Low Returns to Public Consumption: To Spend Poorly Is Like Not Spending

Beyond the issues related to output volatility described in the previous section, one could see the positive in additional expenditure in public spending during good times for countries desperately underprovisioned in basic public goods such as education, health, or security. Even if this spending is downwardly rigid, improvement in the provision of public goods and public investment could help improve productivity and the long-term growth outlook, thus helping mitigate pressures on fiscal sustainability. Unfortunately, the procyclical public spending multipliers in low- and middle-income countries during good times shown in figure 2.4 were positive but small. This may be counterintuitive

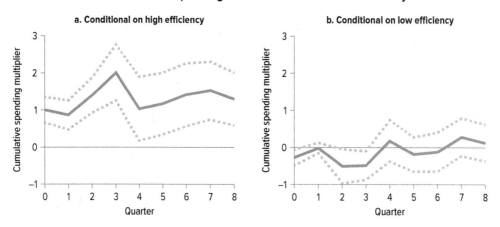

Source: Original calculation based on Izquierdo et al. 2019.
Note: Dashed lines indicate the 95 percent confidence interval for the effect of current expenditure.
See Annex 2A for a definition of the sample of countries.

given the low stocks of these publicly provided goods and services. Beyond the fact that there may be long-run growth effects not captured by spending multipliers, one potential explanation for the low returns on public consumption is rooted in the (in)efficiency of public spending in low- and middle-income markets.

To test this hypothesis, we reestimate the spending multipliers along an efficiency dimension. In other words, we test whether there is a difference in the returns on public consumption among the most and least efficient economies in our sample. Our index of efficiency is based on measures of institutional quality reported by the Global Competitiveness Index between 2006 and 2016. These data integrate the macroeconomic and the microeconomic or business aspects of competitiveness into a single index. A major part of the data set is extracted from the Executive Opinion Survey, which captures responses from a representative sample of business leaders all over the world. Respondent numbers were just over 13,500 in 142 countries for the 2010 survey. Figure 2.4 shows spending multipliers for the most efficient economies (panel a) and those for the least efficient economies (panel b). Efficient economies see relatively large and persistent gains in public consumption. The least efficient economies see no gains at all. The emerging picture is a perfect example of how far returns on public spending in emerging markets are dragged down by inefficient spending.

As shown in panel b, inefficient spending may have the same result as no spending at all. On the flip side, panel a shows that the size of aggregate spending multipliers can be large when public spending is conducted efficiently, with a cumulative multiplier return on primary public spending peaking at almost US$2.00 after one year.

Additional evidence in recent literature suggests that the output effect of public investment in the first two to four years falls when efficiency is low (Cavallo and Daude 2011; Furceri and Li 2017; Izquierdo, Pessino, and Vuletin 2018; Leduc and Wilson 2013; Leeper, Walker, and Yang 2010).

In this chapter, we show that procyclical public consumption tends to accentuate the business cycle, especially in difficult times, leading to increased macroeconomic volatility. In a more novel insight, we illustrate that low- and middle-income markets are semiprocyclical, meaning that they display asymmetric fiscal behavior over the business cycle. In good times, low- and middle-income markets tend to increase public consumption faster than economic growth. Meanwhile, rigidities in public consumption mean that these expansions are not followed by similar contractions during bad times. This ratcheted effect, combined with low returns on public consumption due to inefficient spending, leads to fiscal gaps. Thus, rather than blaming economic contractions, the path to fiscal trouble in low- and middle-income markets may well start with the mismanagement of public spending during good times.

Annex 2A: Categorization of Countries

TABLE 2A.1: **Categorization of Countries in Chapter 2 Figures**

Figure	Category	Countries Included
Figures 2.2 and 2.3	Low- and middle-income markets	Argentina; Bahrain; Bangladesh; Botswana; Brazil; Bulgaria; Chile; China; Colombia; Côte d'Ivoire; Croatia; Cyprus; Czechia; Egypt, Arab Rep.; Estonia; Ghana; Greece; Hungary; Iceland; India; Indonesia; Jamaica; Jordan; Kazakhstan; Kenya; Kuwait; Latvia; Lebanon; Lithuania; Malaysia; Mauritius; Mexico; Morocco; Namibia; Nigeria; Oman; Pakistan; Panama; Peru; Philippines; Poland; Qatar; Romania; Russian Federation; Saudi Arabia; Slovak Republic; Slovenia; South Africa; Sri Lanka; Taiwan; Thailand; Trinidad and Tobago; Tunisia; Türkiye; Ukraine; United Arab Emirates; Viet Nam; and Zambia
	High-income economies	Australia; Austria; Belgium; Canada; Denmark; Finland; France; Germany; Hong Kong SAR, China; Ireland; Israel; Italy; Japan; and Korea, Rep. of.
Figure 2.4	Sample	Albania; Argentina; Australia; Austria; Belgium; Bolivia; Botswana; Brazil; Brunei Darussalam; Bulgaria; Canada; Chile; Colombia; Costa Rica; Croatia; Cyprus; Czechia; Denmark; Dominican Republic; Ecuador; Egypt, Arab Rep.; Estonia; Finland; France; Georgia; Germany; Greece; Guatemala; Honduras; Hong Kong SAR, China; Hungary; Iceland; India; Indonesia; Ireland; Israel; Italy; Japan; Korea, Rep. of; Kyrgyz Republic; Latvia; Lithuania; Luxembourg; Malaysia; Malta; Mauritius; Mexico; Netherlands; New Zealand; Nicaragua; North Macedonia; Norway; Paraguay; Philippines; Poland; Portugal; Romania; Russian Federation; Serbia; Singapore; Slovak Republic; Slovenia; South Africa; Spain; Sweden; Switzerland; Thailand; Türkiye; United Kingdom; United States; Uruguay; and Venezuela, RB

Notes

1. "Big G" refers to the aggregate government expenditure component in the expenditure approach of calculating gross domestic product (GDP). This approach combines the total amount spent on final goods and services within an economy during a particular period, usually a year.

2. The seemingly extreme negative values for the multiplier were explained by large foreign capital retreats following fiscal sustainability fears after the increases in public spending led to larger fiscal deficits.

3. Alternative econometric methods such as system generalized method of moments that use lag structures of the independent variables as instruments were also used and rendered similar results.

References

Alesina, A., R. Baqir, and W. Easterly. 2000. "Redistributive Public Employment." *Journal of Urban Economics* 48 (2): 219–41.

Alesina, A., F. R. Campante, and G. Tabellini. 2008. "Why Is Fiscal Policy Often Procyclical?" *Journal of the European Economic Association* 6 (5): 1006–36.

Ardanaz, M., and A. Izquierdo. 2017. "Current Expenditure Upswings in Good Times and Public Investment Downswings in Bad Times? New Evidence from Developing Countries." *Journal of Comparative Economics* 50 (1): 118–34.

Auerbach, A. J., and Y. Gorodnichenko. 2012. "Measuring the Output Responses to Fiscal Policy." *American Economic Journal: Economic Policy* 4 (2): 1–27.

Auerbach, A. J., and Y. Gorodnichenko. 2013. "Output Spillovers from Fiscal Policy." *American Economic Review* 103 (3): 141–6.

Bachmann, R., and E. R. Sims. 2012. "Confidence and the Transmission of Government Spending Shocks." *Journal of Monetary Economics* 59 (3): 235–49.

Baez, J. E., M. E. Genoni, L. Lucchetti, and M. Salazar. 2017. "Gone with the Storm: Rainfall Shocks and Household Wellbeing in Guatemala." *Journal of Development Studies* 53 (8): 1253–71.

Balassone, F., and M. Francese. 2004. "Cyclical Asymmetry in Fiscal Policy, Debt Accumulation and the Treaty of Maastricht." Working Paper, Banca d'Italia, Rome.

Balassone, F., and M. Kumar. 2007. "Cyclicality of Fiscal Policy." In *Promoting Fiscal Discipline*, edited by M. S. Kumar and T. Ter-Minassian, 19–35. Washington, DC: International Monetary Fund.

Barrot, L. D., C. Calderón, and L. Servén. 2018. "Openness, Specialization, and the External Vulnerability of Developing Countries." *Journal of Development Economics* 134: 310–28.

Caballero, R. J., and A. Krishnamurthy. 2004. "Fiscal Policy and Financial Depth." Working Paper 10532, National Bureau of Economic Research, Cambridge, MA.

Candelon, B., and L. Lieb. 2013. "Fiscal Policy in Good and Bad Times." *Journal of Economic Dynamics and Control* 37 (12): 2679–94.

Carneiro, F., and L. Garrido. 2015. "New Evidence on the Cyclicality of Fiscal Policy." Policy Research Working Paper 7293, World Bank, Washington, DC.

Cavallo, E., and C. Daude. 2011. "Public Investment in Developing Countries: A Blessing or a Curse?" *Journal of Comparative Economics* 39 (1): 65–81.

Céspedes, L. F., and A. Velasco. 2014. "Was This Time Different? Fiscal Policy in Commodity Republics." *Journal of Development Economics* 106: 92–106.

Cetrángolo, O., J. P. Jiménez, and R. Ruiz de Castillo. 2010. *Rigidities and Fiscal Space in Latin America: A Comparative Case Study*. Vitacura, Chile: Economic Commission for Latin America and the Caribbean.

Echeverry, J. C., J. A. Bonilla, and A. Moya. 2006. "Rigideces institucionales y flexibilidad presupuestaria: Los casos de Argentina, Colombia, México y Perú." Documentos CEDE 3475, Universidad de los Andes, Bogotá.

Frankel, J. A., C. A. Vegh, and G. Vuletin. 2013. "On Graduation from Fiscal Procyclicality." *Journal of Development Economics* 100 (1): 32–47.

Furceri, D., and B. G. Li. 2017. *The Macroeconomic (and Distributional) Effects of Public Investment in Developing Economies*. Washington, DC: International Monetary Fund.

Gavin, M., R. Hausmann, R. Perotti, and E. Talvi. 1996. "Managing Fiscal Policy in Latin America and the Caribbean: Volatility, Procyclicality, and Limited Creditworthiness." Working Paper 326, Inter-American Development Bank, Washington, DC.

Gavin, M., and R. Perotti. 1997. "Fiscal Policy in Latin America." *NBER Macroeconomics Annual* 12: 11–61.

Hercowitz, Z., and M. Strawczynski. 2004. "Cyclical Ratcheting in Government Spending: Evidence from the OECD." *Review of Economics and Statistics* 86 (1): 353–61.

Herrera, S., and E. Olaberria. 2020. *Budget Rigidity in Latin America and the Caribbean: Causes, Consequences, and Policy Implications.* International Development in Focus. Washington, DC: World Bank.

Huidrom, R., M. A. Kose, J. J. Lim, and F. L. Ohnsorge. 2020. "Why Do Fiscal Multipliers Depend on Fiscal Positions?" *Journal of Monetary Economics* 114: 109–25. https://doi .org/10.1016/j.jmoneco.2019.03.004

Humphreys, M., and M. E. Sandbu. 2007. "The Political Economy of Natural Resource Funds." In *Escaping the Resource Curse,* edited by M. Humphreys, J. D. Sachs, and J. E. Stiglitz, 194–233. New York: Columbia University Press.

Ilzetzki, E. 2011. "Rent-Seeking Distortions and Fiscal Procyclicality." *Journal of Development Economics* 96 (1): 30–46.

Ilzetzki, E., E. G. Mendoza, and C. A. Végh. 2013. "How Big (Small?) Are Fiscal Multipliers?" *Journal of Monetary Economics* 60 (2): 239–54.

Ilzetzki, E., and C. A. Végh. 2008. "Procyclical Fiscal Policy in Developing Countries: Truth or Fiction?" Working Paper 14191, National Bureau of Economic Research, Cambridge, MA.

Izquierdo, A., R. E. Lama, J. P. Medina, J. P. Puig, D. Riera-Crichton, C. A. Vegh, and G. Vuletin. 2019. "Is the Public Investment Multiplier Higher in Developing Countries? An Empirical Investigation." Working Paper 26478, National Bureau of Economic Research, Cambridge, MA.

Izquierdo, A., C. Pessino, and G. Vuletin, eds. 2018. *Better Spending for Better Lives: How Latin America and the Caribbean Can Do More with Less.* Vol. 10. Washington, DC: Inter-American Development Bank.

Jaimovich, D., and U. Panizza. 2007. *Procyclicality or Reverse Causality?* Washington, DC: Inter-American Development Bank.

Kaminsky, G. L., C. M. Reinhart, and C. A. Végh. 2004. "When It Rains, It Pours: Procyclical Capital Flows and Macroeconomic Policies." *NBER Macroeconomics Annual* 19: 11–53.

Lane, P. R. 2003. "The Cyclical Behaviour of Fiscal Policy: Evidence from the OECD." *Journal of Public Economics* 87 (12): 2661–75.

Leduc, S., and D. Wilson. 2013. "Roads to Prosperity or Bridges to Nowhere? Theory and Evidence on the Impact of Public Infrastructure Investment." *NBER Macroeconomics Annual* 27: 89–142.

Leeper, E. M., T. B. Walker, and S. C. S. Yang. 2010. "Government Investment and Fiscal Stimulus." *Journal of Monetary Economics* 57 (8): 1000–12.

Loayza, N. V., and I. Otker-Robe. 2014. *World Development Report: Risk and Opportunity— Managing Risk for Development.* Washington, DC: World Bank.

Loayza, N. V., R. Rancière, L. Servén, and J. Ventura. 2007. "Macroeconomic Volatility and Welfare in Developing Countries: An Introduction." *World Bank Economic Review* 21 (3): 343–57.

Mendoza, E. G., and P. Oviedo. 2006. "Fiscal Policy and Macroeconomic Uncertainty in Developing Countries." Working Paper 12586, National Bureau of Economic Research, Cambridge, MA.

Ostrom, E. 1990. *Governing the Commons: The Evolution of Institutions for Collective Action.* Cambridge: Cambridge University Press.

Owyang, M. T., V. A. Ramey, and S. Zubairy. 2013. "Are Government Spending Multipliers Greater during Periods of Slack? Evidence from Twentieth-Century Historical Data." *American Economic Review* 103 (3): 129–34.

Raddatz, C. 2008. *Have External Shocks Become More Important for Output Fluctuations in African Countries?* In *Africa at a Turning Point? Growth, Aid, and External Shocks*, edited by D. S. Go and J. Page, 343–73. Washington, DC: World Bank.

Riascos, A., and C. A. Vegh. 2003. *Procyclical Government Spending in Developing Countries: The Role of Capital Market Imperfections.* Washington, DC: International Monetary Fund.

Riera-Crichton, D., C. A. Vegh, and G. Vuletin. 2015. "Procyclical and Countercyclical Fiscal Multipliers: Evidence from OECD Countries." *Journal of International Money and Finance* 52: 15–31.

Rigobon, R. 2004. "When It Rains, It Pours: Procyclical Capital Flows and Macroeconomic Policies: Comment." *NBER Macroeconomics Annual* 19: 62–79.

Rodrik, D. 2000. "Institutions for High-Quality Growth: What They Are and How to Acquire Them." *Studies in Comparative International Development* 35 (3): 3–31.

Talvi, E., and C. A. Végh. 2005. "Tax Base Variability and Procyclical Fiscal Policy in Developing Countries." *Journal of Development Economics* 78 (1): 156–90.

Tornell, A., and P. R. Lane. 1999. "The Voracity Effect." *American Economic Review* 89 (1): 22–46.

Vegh, C. A., G. Vuletin, D. Riera-Crichton, J. P. Medina, D. Friedheim, L. Morano, and L. Venturi. 2018. *From Known Unknowns to Black Swans: How to Manage Risk in Latin America and the Caribbean.* Washington, DC: World Bank.

Velasco, A. 1997. "When Are Fixed Exchange Rates Really Fixed?" *Journal of Development Economics* 54 (1): 5–25.

3

In "Bad Times," Lack of Automatic Stabilizers Leads to Good Intentions with "Too"-Rigid Outcomes

Introduction

When hit by an economic recession, high-income economies rely on automatic spending to provide economic support to those in need during trying times. This countercyclical public spending helps reactivate consumption and prevents families from falling into poverty. Although the need for economic stabilizers during recessions is also shared by low- and middle-income markets, the fiscal tools available in these countries are different. Widespread informality in labor markets makes the archetypal automatic stabilizer, unemployment insurance, infeasible in low- and middle-income markets. Without unemployment insurance, low- and middle-income markets resort to expanding social transfers such as conditional cash transfers (CCTs), which include incentives for employment, education, and housing for poor and vulnerable households. The key difference between these countercyclical support efforts resides in the rigidity of the fiscal tools. Although unemployment insurance is flexible by construction—that is, it increases as unemployment rises in bad times and then decreases as households regain access to the labor market—CCTs tend to be downwardly rigid by nature.[1] Because these social transfers were conceived to address structural poverty issues, not business cycle problems, governments find it very difficult to cut back on them once the economy starts to improve.

Social security represents one-third of all government primary spending in low- and middle-income economies. This category alone represents 80 percent of all the so-called automatic spending in low- and middle-income countries and matches the size of public consumption. Moreover, given falling birth rates and the aging population, it is expected (in the absence of social security reforms) that social security spending could grow between two- and fivefold in the next 40 years (for example, Bongaarts 2004; Nerlich and Schroth 2018; Panadeiros and Pessino 2018). Expanding social transfers in countries with a large share of vulnerable households during bad times boosts economic activity in the short run, thus helping to mitigate the effects of the recession. Nonetheless, the economic returns of these social transfers are relatively small and short-lived, which leads to fiscal stress as countries struggle to pay back their fiscal efforts. As was the case with public consumption in good times, the downward rigidity of these expenditures ties the structural size of the public sector to short-run fluctuations in the business cycle.

Lack of Effective Unemployment Insurance Means No Automatic Stabilizers in Bad Times

As we have shown, low- and middle-income markets clearly suffer from procyclicality in the overall primary balance. When looking at the cyclicality of the components of public spending, the literature has mainly focused on government consumption and government investment (for example, Ardanaz and Izquierdo 2017; Ilzetzki and Végh 2008; Izquierdo, Pessino, and Vuletin 2018; Kaminsky, Reinhart, and Végh 2004; Talvi and Vegh 2005). In the previous chapter, we showed how public consumption (which includes mainly wages and salaries and purchases of goods and services) tends to be acyclical in high-income countries and procyclical (and downwardly rigid) in low- and middle-income economies. As to government investment, studies have shown it to be countercyclical in high-income economies and procyclical in low- and middle-income countries (see Ardanaz and Izquierdo 2017; Izquierdo, Pessino, and Vuletin 2018). Nonetheless, both government consumption and government investment are raised in their majority from deliberate spending decisions by policy makers during the approval of their annual budgets. Much less focus has been put on the cyclical behavior of automatic spending, that is, the spending not directly related to discretionary decisions from policy makers. Automatic spending typically involves the disbursement of public funds resulting from laws (and even constitutional mandates) benefiting individuals who meet certain eligibility criteria. The specific nature and type of social programs are, naturally, shaped by countries' most pressing social challenges. The most important automatic spending categories include unemployment insurance (transfers to unemployed individuals), CCTs and benefits mainly to poor individuals and the most vulnerable households, and social security (mainly transfers to individuals after retirement).

Of these three main components of automatic spending, unemployment insurance has been a source of countercyclicality for high-income and low- and middle-income economies alike. As shown in figure 3.1, similar levels of negative correlation between unemployment insurance spending and the business cycle (countercyclicality) can be observed in high-income and low- and middle-income countries. As an automatic stabilizer, in bad times unemployment grows and more workers meet the criteria, so unemployment insurance payments increase. In good times, as employment recovers, unemployment benefits decrease.

FIGURE 3.1: Unemployment Insurance Is a Key Automatic Stabilizer

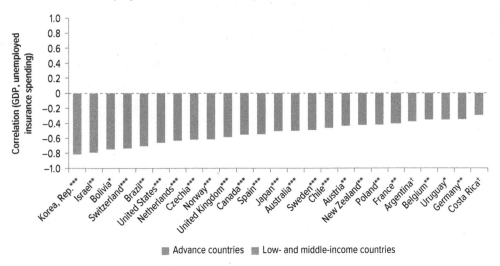

Source: Galeano et al. 2021, based on Red de Centros (Inter-American Development Bank) for Argentina, Bolivia, Brazil, Costa Rica, and Uruguay and Organisation for Economic Co-operation and Development for the remaining countries.

Note: Sample of 25 countries for period 1980–2015 based on data availability. The cyclical components have been estimated using the Hodrick-Prescott filter. A positive correlation indicates procyclical unemployment insurance spending; a negative correlation, countercyclical unemployment insurance spending. Correlations are pooled across countries. Real unemployment insurance spending is defined as unemployment insurance spending, deflated by the GDP deflator. GDP = gross domestic product.

$^{\dagger}p < .15. *p < .10. **p < .05. ***p < .10.$

However, in contrast to low- and middle-income countries' long history of social protection in terms of social security and the most recent wave of family programs, particularly CCTs, unemployment insurance programs are uncommon in these economies. Typically, they simply do not exist, or, if they do, they have negligible coverage.

Map 3.1 shows whether unemployment insurance mechanisms are present or absent in every country in the world. All high-income countries have unemployment insurance, typically dating back to the Great Depression of 1929–39. In contrast, only 40 percent (or 43 of 109) of low- and middle-income countries currently have some sort of unemployment insurance mechanism. This includes highly ineffective measures such as unemployment indemnities that firms have to pay just as they head toward bankruptcy.

Beyond the existence of an unemployment insurance scheme, the problem many low- and middle-income countries face is their effective deployment. To showcase this challenge, and using data from the International Labour Organization and Aleksynska and Schindler (2011), Galeano et al. (2021) create a measure of effective unemployment insurance mechanism coverage, defined as the product of the extensive margin (that is, the ratio of unemployed individuals covered by the unemployment insurance program) and the intensive margin (defined by the gross replacement rate, which is specified as the ratio of unemployment insurance benefits a worker receives relative to the worker's last gross earning). This effective measure ranges between 0 (no income replacement for any unemployed workers) and 100 (all unemployed workers receive a benefit equal to their last income).

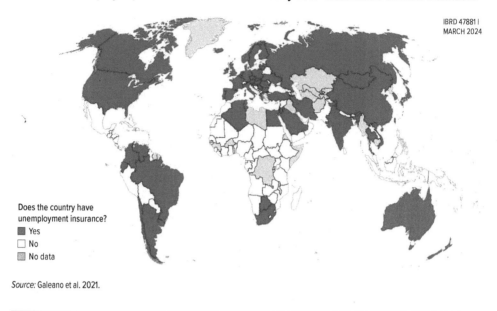

Does the country have
unemployment insurance?
■ Yes
☐ No
▨ No data

Source: Galeano et al. 2021.

FIGURE 3.2: **Effective Coverage of Unemployment Insurance Programs**

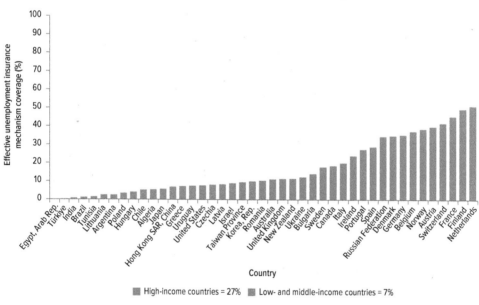

■ High-income countries = 27% ■ Low- and middle-income countries = 7%

Source: Galeano et al. 2021.

This new measure is presented in figure 3.2 for countries with some unemployment insurance mechanism. In low- and middle-income countries, the effective unemployment insurance mechanism coverage is 7 percent, statistically significantly lower than that of high-income countries, which is about four times larger (27 percent). In other words, although about 40 percent of low- and middle-income countries do have some unemployment insurance programs, their effective coverage is (unlike that in high-income countries) negligible.

Furthermore, by decomposing the extensive and intensive margins, panels a and b of figure 3.3 show that the problem resides in coverage (extensive margin), where the differences between high-income countries and low- and middle-income countries are truly stark. Although 60 percent of employees are covered by the unemployment insurance program in high-income economies, fewer than half (23 percent) are covered in low- and middle-income economies.

The critical question is, thus, Why do low- and middle-income countries lag behind in the provision of such an important shock absorber as unemployment insurance? The answer is particularly relevant for these countries, given that they are inherently more volatile than their high-income counterparts.

A key mechanism behind these differences is the presence of a large informal economy (Asenjo and Pignatti 2019; Bosch and Esteban-Pretel 2015; Duval and Loungani 2019; Fiess, Fugazza, and Maloney 2010; Maloney 2004; Perry et al. 2007). A large informal share of workers makes unemployment insurance impractical because of moral hazard considerations, because unemployed individuals may work in the informal sector while receiving unemployment insurance benefits (Alvarez-Parra and Sanchez 2009; Hopenhayn and Nicolini 1997). Specifically, if workers can accept jobs in the informal sector while continuing to receive unemployment insurance benefits without being detected by the government, a more generous unemployment insurance system would reduce the incentive to search for a formal job and induce workers to accept informal jobs (Gonzalez-Rozada and Ruffo 2016). Indeed, figure 3.4 shows, using cross-sectional data for 41 countries with some type of unemployment insurance program, that higher informality is strongly associated with lower effective unemployment insurance coverage. It is also the case that many low- and middle-income markets have a type of unemployment indemnity that is hard to replace for political economy reasons.

Interestingly, and in line with the proposed logic, the degree of informality in countries without any type of unemployment insurance mechanism is much larger than that observed in countries with unemployment insurance (even those in low- and middle-income countries). For example, using 2010 data, countries without unemployment insurance have an informal sector twice as large as that of countries with some sort of unemployment insurance mechanism (36 percent compared with 18 percent, with the difference being statistically significant).

In sum, although unemployment insurance programs work in practice as predicted by theory (that is, countercyclically) in both low- and middle-income and high-income countries, the absence, or negligible coverage, of such programs in low- and middle-income countries helps to explain the lack of countercyclicality observed in automatic spending in those countries.

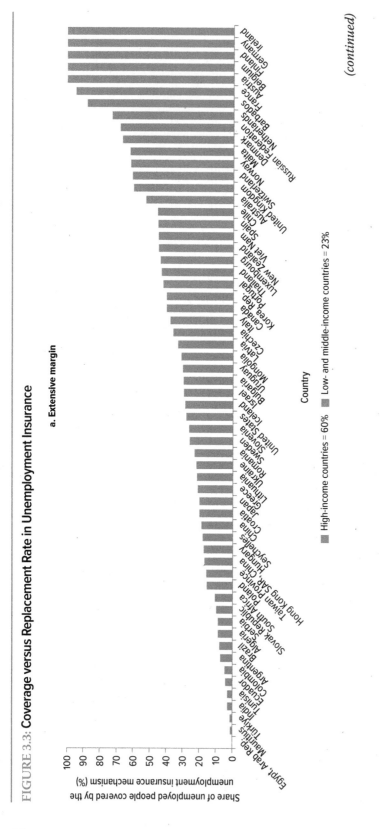

FIGURE 3.3: Coverage versus Replacement Rate in Unemployment Insurance

a. Extensive margin

(continued)

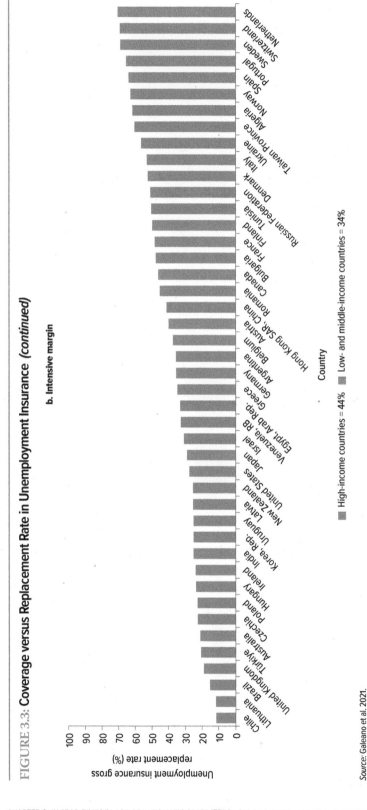

FIGURE 3.3: Coverage versus Replacement Rate in Unemployment Insurance *(continued)*

b. Intensive margin

Source: Galeano et al. 2021.

FIGURE 3.4: Effective Unemployment Insurance versus Informality

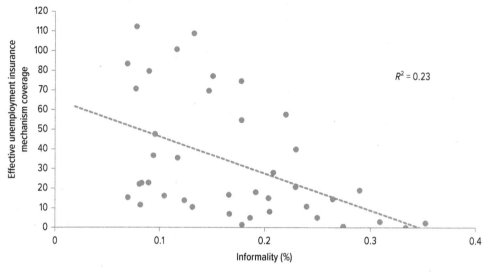

Source: Galeano et al. 2021.

Note: Effective unemployment insurance mechanism coverage = 0.3***[5.5]−0.9***[−4.1] × Informality. R^2 = 0.23. Numbers in brackets represent the *t* statistic.

***significant at 99 percent.

In "Bad Times," Good Intentions with "Too"-Rigid Outcomes

Low- and middle-income markets, especially middle-income countries in Latin America and the Caribbean (LAC), have a long history of social protection. As shown in the previous section, the lack of effective automatic stabilizers forces these low- and middle-income nations to increase other types of social transfer. Specifically, in bad times, low- and middle-income nations tend to expand social security through family programs, particularly CCTs.

Social transfers encompass both ongoing social protection programs and emergency policy responses. *Ongoing social protection programs* refers to the disbursement of government funds to individuals who meet certain eligibility criteria. The main categories include unemployment benefits, family programs, and pensions. Overall, social transfers have been increasing continuously over time, mainly because of the impact of aging populations on pensions as well as a consequence of expanding family programs targeting the poor and most vulnerable households (especially in the low- and middle-income countries). Family programs and more general CCT programs had a significant role in shaping social policy in Latin America over the past two decades. Conditional transfer programs have been spreading rapidly since the mid-1990s. They started in Brazil (Bolsa Familia) and Mexico (Oportunidades; before that, Progresa), and by 2016 there were 30 active programs in 20 countries in the region, covering almost 17 percent of all households (see Cecchini and Atuesta 2017). These poverty-targeted government initiatives aim to include populations traditionally excluded from social protection services by coordinating intersectoral actions in education, health, and nutrition. CCT programs use innovative management models, moving away from traditional clientelistic mechanisms. They modernize social policy through technological innovations such as beneficiary registries and information management systems.

Although, on average, social transfers account for more than 50 percent of primary government spending in high-income countries and about 40 percent in low- and middle-income countries (Galeano et al. 2021), their role in low- and middle-income markets is modest compared with that of the Organisation for Economic Co-operation and Development (OECD; Atkinson 2003). In a recent report, the World Bank showed that in LAC in the 2000s, taxes and transfers created a little wedge between the market-determined Gini and that of disposable income after tax and transfer. By contrast, the "pre-fiscal" EU15 Gini of 0.47 fell by 14 percentage points to 0.33 after taxes and transfers. Fully half of the difference in disposable income inequality between Latin America and Europe (or the United States) was attributable to the different effectiveness of tax-and-transfer systems (Perry et al. 2006). More recent studies focusing on family programs and CCTs show that, despite uneven outcomes across the regions, there is a positive effect on human capacity, education, health care, growth, preventive health check-ups, child nutrition, income levels, poverty indicators, and consumption. Additionally, evidence suggests that CCT programs contribute to reductions in child labor and empower mothers. Despite these positive outcomes, CCTs face harsh criticism, with some CCT programs not addressing structural poverty factors while being exploited by the elites (political and economic groups with some degree of institutional control and legislative power) for political and welfare purposes. Other critiques highlight operational challenges.[2]

Despite these distributional and efficiency issues, discretionary public transfers to households and firms to secure employment were critical to cushion the economic impact of the COVID-19 crisis. At the same time, when OECD countries used some of the largest emergency social transfers in history as policy responses to COVID-19,[3] low- and middle-income markets also adopted sizable social protection programs to cushion the impact of the COVID-19 crisis. In LAC, for example, 30 countries mobilized additional resources for social assistance. Seven countries in the LAC region expanded resources for social insurance, and another two added resources for labor market interventions. Taken together these new interventions expanded the reach of social transfers from less than one-third of the population to a full two-thirds of it. This puts the LAC region on par with East Asia and the Pacific in terms of overall population coverage of stimulus programs, ahead of all other low- and middle-income regions.[4]

The average transfer per person was generally smaller in LAC than in other middle-income regions, but the number of persons benefiting was much higher. In Bolivia and Peru, for example, the ambition was to cover 90 percent of the population.

Around the world, implementation challenges mean that not all targeted households received an adequate level of relief, and assessing actual coverage is difficult. By one estimate, some of the largest programs in practice are the Bono Familia and Bono Universal programs in Bolivia, which effectively reach 54 percent of the population; the Quedate en Casa program in the Dominican Republic (49 percent); the Ingreso Familiar de Emergencia and Bono de Emergencia in Chile (34 percent); the Auxilio Emergencial in Brazil (31 percent); and the Bono 380 in Peru (30 percent). The absolute number of beneficiaries of these emergency programs is large enough for five countries in the region—Brazil, Peru, Colombia, Argentina, and Chile, in that order—to be among the largest 10 in the low- and middle-income world (Gentilini et al. 2020). In the case of Brazil, the scale of the program was such that, despite the economic downturn, the poverty rate is estimated to have dropped below its precrisis level. World Bank simulations suggest that with the final expansion of the government's emergency cash transfer program in Brazil (among other fiscal measures), the fraction of the population living on less than US$5.50 per day (in purchasing power parity prices of 2011) could be below 14 percent, compared with 19.7 percent a year earlier.

The importance of social transfers is reflected in the breakdown of public spending by category under the stimulus packages adopted in response to the crisis. Spending can be classified as funding the health care response, helping households, supporting businesses, and other efforts that are difficult to map to any single objective. In four countries in the region, social transfers accounted for more than half of the package, reaching more than three-quarters in the case of Panama. Five other countries devoted between 40 and 50 percent of their fiscal stimulus to assisting households (figure 3.5).

We address the effectiveness (in terms of output and social returns) of these social transfers in the next chapter, but a crucial characteristic of this type of public spending is, similar to public consumption in good times, its downward rigidity. In other words, once the social transfer is imposed, the way these transfers are structured and monitored and strong political economy arguments make them very difficult to reverse. Figure 3.6 provides an example of how this downward rigidity looks using Argentina and Mexico as

FIGURE 3.5: Social Transfers in Latin America and the Caribbean during COVID-19

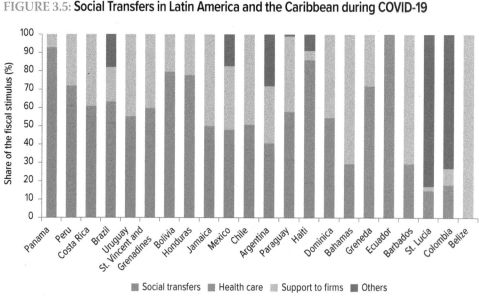

Source: World Bank 2020.

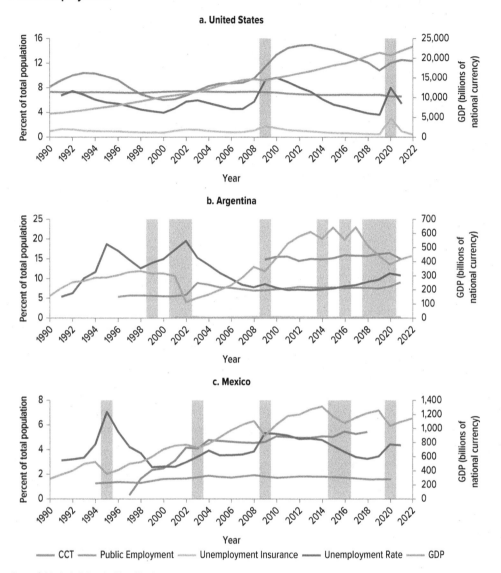

FIGURE 3.6: **Downwardly Rigid Increases in Conditional Cash Transfers and Public Employment**

a. United States

b. Argentina

c. Mexico

CCT —— Public Employment —— Unemployment Insurance —— Unemployment Rate —— GDP

Source: Original calculations for this publication.

Note: Areas shaded in gray represent recessions. CCT = conditional cash transfers; GDP = gross domestic product.

the low- and middle-income markets representatives and the United States as a high-income economy, all of which have relatively large CCT programs. In all recessions (shaded areas), CCTs increase across the board, effectively working as a countercyclical policy and helping to lessen the effects of lower income on households. In contrast to the United States, where CCT spending decreased during economic recoveries, CCTs in Argentina and Mexico did not diminish, becoming acyclical in the good times.

This downward rigidity leads to a large accumulation of liabilities over time, essentially reducing the fiscal space of the public sector.

Figure 3.6 also shows the use of employment policies as an alternative to CCTs to compensate for the lack of unemployment insurance. Whereas public employment in the United States is relatively uncorrelated to the business cycle, the same is not true in Argentina and, in a lesser way, Mexico. In both countries, but especially in Argentina before the establishment of CCTs, public employment acts as a shock absorber in the absence of unemployment insurance. As with CCTs, public employment in both countries seems to be sticky and comes down only slowly during the recoveries, typically staying at higher levels than before the recession.

Countercyclical in Bad Times: Effective in the Short Run but Costly in the Long Run

Chapter 2 showed how the lack of effective automatic stabilizers (especially unemployment insurance) pushes low- and middle-income economies to use social transfers, typically in the shape of CCTs as countercyclical fiscal policy instruments during bad times in their efforts to help households and firms during bad times. Although, as we have learned, the rigidity of these instruments may lead to fiscal distress down the road, it is also important to evaluate their efficiency in helping vulnerable economic groups through the worst part of the economic cycle.

Moreover, the use of alternative fiscal instruments in low- and middle-income countries to cope with the COVID-19 pandemic has redoubled the interest in evaluating the performance of such policies. In this context, the spending multiplier of social transfers is receiving special attention. In other words, we know now that spending composition forces low- and middle-income markets to react to downturns with social transfers, but does that mean that spending composition also affects the impact of cyclical policies?

Social transfers are associated with both ongoing social protection programs and emergency policy responses. Most often they involve the disbursement of public funds, and they target individuals or households who meet certain eligibility criteria. Examples include pensions, unemployment benefits, family allowances, CCTs, and social assistance.

Empirical evidence on the size of social transfer multipliers (STMs)—that is, the effect that each US$1 change in social transfers has on the level of GDP—is relatively recent and primarily based on data from high-income economies. These studies find that the impact of social transfers on economic activity is modest, with one additional unit of spending typically leading to an increase in aggregate output ranging between zero and one (Alesina et al. 2017; Gechert 2015; Gechert, Paetz, and Villanueva 2020; Parraga-Rodriguez 2018). Interestingly, among the few existing papers, there is a strong consensus that social transfer shocks affect output mainly through consumption rather than through investment (Alesina et al. 2017; Gechert, Paetz, and Villanueva 2020; Parraga-Rodriguez 2018; Pennings 2020; Romer and Romer 2016). This empirical fact points out that the primary mechanism behind the social transfer shock occurs through the government allocation of funds to agents with a high marginal propensity to consume, rather than through supply-side channels.

Although much less evidence is presented for low- and middle-income countries, a recent study based on six countries in Latin America (Bracco et al. 2021) finds much larger social transfer multipliers for these middle-income countries than for their high-income counterparts.

Figure 3.7 estimates the impulse responses of output, consumption, and investment to a US$1 shock in government social transfers for LAC and developed countries. Estimates are obtained using the well-known Blanchard and Perotti (2002) identification strategy that imposes timing restrictions by assuming that although government spending changes are allowed to contemporaneously affect economic activity within the quarter, it takes the government at least one quarter to respond to developments in the state of the economy.[5]

The STMs estimated in figure 3.7 show that the size of the STM is three times larger in Latin American countries than in high-income economies. Whereas the STM is, on impact, 0.3 in developed economies, it is 0.9 in Latin American economies. In line with existing empirical papers based on data from developed countries, both samples also show that the effect on output is mainly driven by private consumption, whereas private investment remains largely unchanged. Of consequence for our analysis of long-term growth, although the macroeconomic impact of social transfers is significant in the short and medium term, it tends to weaken in the long term.

But why are STMs so much larger in low- and middle-income nations? The answer seems to lay in the large differences in social structure across low- and middle-income and high-income nations. In particular, using a calibrated two-agent new Keynesian (TANK) model (refer to Box 3.1 for a brief description of these types of models), Bracco et al. (2021) find that the gap in STMs between high-income and low- and middle-income markets can be explained almost entirely by differences in the share of households who live from hand to mouth (HtM).

Two findings stand out from several interesting ones. First, as shown in figure 3.8, the share of HtM individuals is larger in low- and middle-income markets than in high-income nations. In this figure, orange bars depict low- and middle-income markets and blue bars indicate high-income countries. For ease of reading, countries with labels correspond to those used in our sample of six Latin American and 17 high-income countries used in the estimation of the impulse responses from figure 3.7. The visual impression is striking: a majority of blue bars lay to the left of the figure and a majority of orange bars lay to the right (indicating a larger share of HtM individuals in low- and middle-income countries). The average share of HtM individuals is twice as large in low- and middle-income countries as in high-income countries (47.5 percent vs. 23.8 percent, with a statistically significant difference). For the sample of six Latin American countries, the average share of HtM individuals is even larger, reaching 60 percent.

FIGURE 3.7: Social Transfer Multipliers: Empirical Estimation for Latin American and High-Income Countries

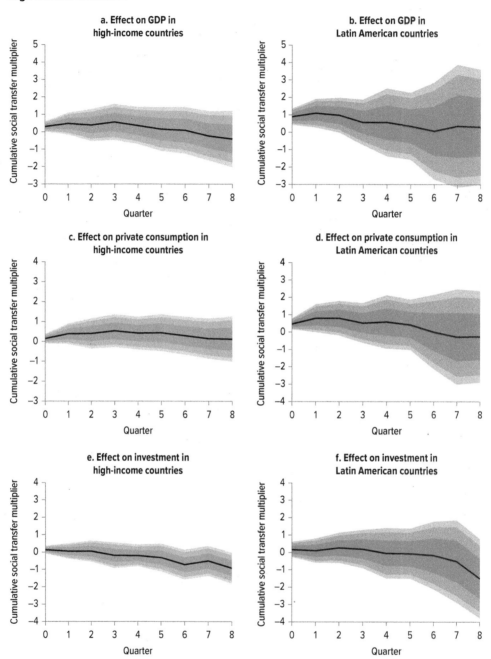

Source: Bracco et al. 2021.

Note: Estimations based on quarterly data for the period 1960–2019 for six Latin American countries (Argentina, Brazil, Chile, Colombia, Mexico, and Peru) and 17 high-income countries (Austria, Belgium, Denmark, Finland, France, Germany, Greece, Ireland, Italy, Luxembourg, Netherlands, Norway, Portugal, Spain, Sweden, United Kingdom, and United States). The social transfer multiplier measures the effect of a US$1 change in social transfers on the level of gross domestic product (panels a and b), consumption (panels c and d), and investment (panels e and f). Dark, medium, and light areas show standard errors at 68, 90, and 95 percent confidence intervals, respectively.

FIGURE 3.8: **Country Share of Hand-to-Mouth Individuals**

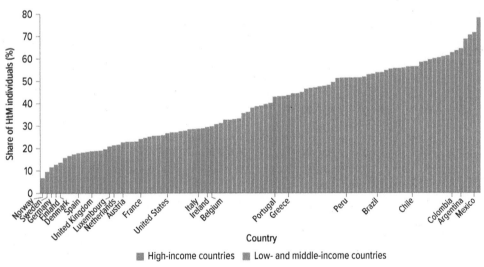

Source: Bracco et al. 2021 based on Global Findex database.
Note: HtM = hand to mouth.

FIGURE 3.9: Country Share of Social Transfers Reaching Hand-to-Mouth Individuals

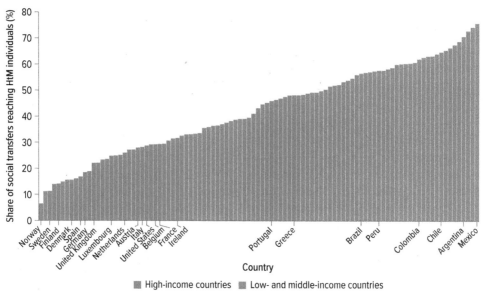

Source: Bracco et al. 2021 based on Global Findex database.
Note: HtM = hand to mouth.

FIGURE 3.10: Share of Hand-to-Mouth and Social Transfer Targeting

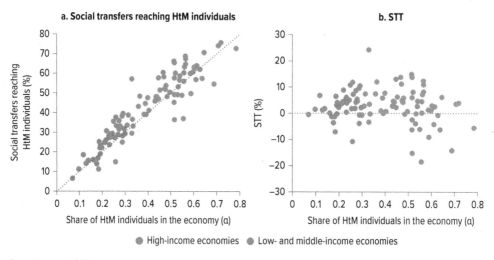

Source: Bracco et al. 2021.
Note: STT is calculated using the formula $\Theta - \alpha$, where Θ = the share of social transfers reaching HtM individuals and α = the share of HtM individuals. HtM = hand to mouth; STT = social transfer targeting.

Second, as shown in figure 3.9, a much larger share of social transfers reach HtM individuals in low- and middle-income countries. The average share of social transfers reaching HtM individuals is about twice as large in low- and middle-income countries as it is in high-income countries (45.7 percent vs. 23.4 percent, with a statistically significant difference). For the sample of six Latin American countries, the average share of social transfers reaching HtM individuals is even larger, reaching 64.6 percent.

Figure 3.10 explains this puzzle. On the one hand, panel a shows that there is a strong relationship between the share of HtM individuals (*x* axis) and the share of social transfers reaching HtM individuals (*y* axis) for most countries, both high income and low and middle income. On the other hand, panel b shows no systematic relationship between social transfer targeting, defined as the share of social transfers reaching HtM individuals minus the total share of HtM individuals in the economy. This is to say that, when considering the universe of all types of social transfers, countries' ability to reach HtM individuals seems to mainly reflect the prevalence of HtM individuals as opposed to a distinct fiscal targeting effort aimed at reaching HtM individuals beyond their representation in the overall population.

Therefore, social transfers in low- and middle-income markets can reach those HtM individuals mainly because a large part of their population is in the HtM group as opposed to a particularly exceptional targeting of social transfers. The same lack of evidence of high-quality social transfer targeting holds also true in developed countries.

Finally, figure 3.11 compares impact multipliers from calibrating the TANK model (orange bars) with the empirical estimates shown in figure 3.7. Interestingly, the TANK model, which is mainly driven by differences in the share of HtM individuals, is able to largely account for the observed empirical evidence. The TANK model delivers much larger STMs for the Latin American sample than for the high-income one. The quantitative STM delivered by the model on impact is 0.21 in high-income countries and 0.92 in the Latin American sample. Notably, these results are well within the reported 90 percent statistical range associated with the empirical STM estimates, which are associated

FIGURE 3.11: Social Transfer Multipliers: Empirical Estimation versus Model Quantitative Results

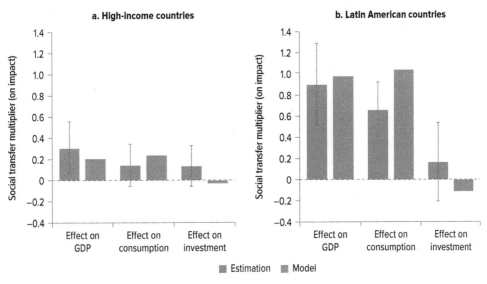

Source: Bracco et al. 2021.

Note: Error bars depict 90 percent confidence intervals. GDP = gross domestic product.

with STM point estimates of 0.31 in high-income countries and 0.90 in the Latin American sample. As observed in the empirical estimates, most of the macroeconomic effect of the social transfer shock is driven by the reaction of private consumption as opposed to private investment. In other words, much like the findings of papers focused on developed countries, the effect on output mainly occurs through consumption, whereas private investment remains virtually unchanged.

Bracco et al. (2021) show how a "bad" initial condition, chronic among low- and middle-income nations, and a relatively large share of financially constrained individuals can lead to larger STMs and thus more effective countercyclical interventions through social transfers in low- and middle-income nations. A larger share of individuals living HtM causes social transfer shocks to easily reach individuals with a high marginal propensity to consume, which, in turn, increases aggregate consumption and output. For this reason, the effect on output is mainly driven by consumption, whereas investment remains mostly unchanged.

Two reflections emerge from this analysis, especially when translating our findings into fiscal policy action. First, given the large size that the STM can achieve, especially in low- and middle-income markets, social transfers emerge as a natural fiscal policy tool to help vulnerable families who are financially constrained and, at the same time, help the economy to recover faster. In this sense, social transfers seem to provide an inclusive manner to deal with temporary and deep recessions, such as during the COVID-19 pandemic. Second, because most of the effect of a social transfer shock affects the economy, especially in the short and medium run (as opposed to having truly long-lasting effects) and through private consumption (as opposed to via increasing the economy's productive capacity and investment), this type of fiscal policy tool is far from ideal to increase long-term growth and productivity.

Notes

1. Ultimately, the countercyclicality of unemployment insurance programs may depend on how they are financed. In American states, for example, higher unemployment means higher charges on businesses.

2. See Cecchini and Madariaga (2011) and Cecchini and Martínez (2011) for a review of the literature.

3. For example, the first phase of the Coronavirus Aid, Relief, and Economic Security Act in the United States included one-time tax rebates to individuals, expanded unemployment benefits, and the Supplemental Nutrition Assistance Program social transfers that represented about US$586 billion, or 2.8 percent of the gross domestic product (GDP) of 2019. This amount is similar to that spent on the American Recovery and Reinvestment Act of 2009 (Oh and Reis 2012).

4. It is worth noting that level of spending and coverage could be different across regions. Although LAC spends more in social transfers than East Asia, the level of coverage is similar. This may be due to better targeting among East Asian economies.

5. To guarantee the unanticipated within-the-quarter nature of the social transfer shock in the context of a local projections approach (Jorda 2005; Stock and Watson 2007), future cumulative changes on social transfers are instrumented at each time horizon $t + h$ using the residual at time t of a regression of changes in social transfers (excluding the unemployment insurance spending component) on the lags of a long list of macroeconomic variables, including the changes of social transfers, GDP, total primary spending, fiscal revenues, and central bank interest rates. The unemployment insurance spending

component is excluded from the social transfer metric used as instrument because it is inherently automatic and reacts quickly to developments in the state of the economy (Di Maggio and Kermani 2016; Galeano et al. 2021; McKay and Reis 2016).

References

Aleksynska, M. M., and M. M. Schindler. 2011. *Labor Market Regulations in Low-, Middle- and High-Income Countries: A New Panel Database*. Washington, DC: International Monetary Fund.

Alesina, A., O. Barbiero, C. Favero, F. Giavazzi, and M. Paradisi. 2017. "The Effects of Fiscal Consolidations: Theory and Evidence." Working Paper 23385, National Bureau of Economic Research, Cambridge, MA.

Alvarez-Parra, F., and J. M. Sanchez. 2009. "Unemployment Insurance with a Hidden Labor Market." *Journal of Monetary Economics* 56 (7): 954–67.

Ardanaz, M., and A. Izquierdo. 2017. "Current Expenditure Upswings in Good Times and Public Investment Downswings in Bad Times? New Evidence from Developing Countries." *Journal of Comparative Economics* 50 (1): 118–34.

Asenjo, A., and C. Pignatti. 2019. *Unemployment Insurance Schemes around the World: Evidence and Policy Options*. Geneva: International Labour Office.

Atkinson, A. B. 2003. "Income Inequality in OECD Countries: Data and Explanations." *CESifo Economic Studies* 49 (4): 479–513.

Blanchard, O., and R. Perotti. 2002. "An Empirical Characterization of the Dynamic Effects of Changes in Government Spending and Taxes on Output." *Quarterly Journal of Economics* 117 (4): 1329–68.

Bongaarts, J. 2004. "Population Aging and the Rising Cost of Public Pensions." *Population and Development Review* 30 (1): 1–23.

Bosch, M., and J. Esteban-Pretel. 2015. "The Labor Market Effects of Introducing Unemployment Benefits in an Economy with High Informality." *European Economic Review* 75: 1–17.

Bracco, J., L. Galeano, D. Riera-Crichton, P. Juarros, and G. Vuletin. 2021. "Social Transfer Multipliers in Developed and Emerging Countries: The Role of Hand-to-Mouth Consumers." Policy Research Working Paper 9627, World Bank, Washington, DC.

Cecchini, S., and B. Atuesta. 2017. *Conditional Cash Transfer Programmes in Latin America and the Caribbean: Coverage and Investment Trends*. Social Policy Series 224. Santiago, Chile: United Nations Economic Commission for Latin America and the Caribbean.

Cecchini, S., and A. Madariaga. 2011. *Conditional Cash Transfer Programmes: The Recent Experience in Latin America and the Caribbean*. Santiago, Chile: United Nations Economic Commission for Latin America and the Caribbean.

Cecchini, S., and R. Martínez. 2011. *Inclusive Social Protection in Latin America: A Comprehensive, Rights-Based Approach*. Santiago, Chile: United Nations Economic Commission for Latin America and the Caribbean.

Di Maggio, M., and A. Kermani. 2016. "The Importance of Unemployment Insurance as an Automatic Stabilizer." Working Paper 22625, National Bureau of Economic Research, Cambridge, MA.

Duval, M. R. A., and M. P. Loungani. 2019. *Designing Labor Market Institutions in Emerging and Developing Economies: Evidence and Policy Options*. Washington, DC: International Monetary Fund.

Fiess, N. M., M. Fugazza, and W. F. Maloney. 2010. "Informal Self-Employment and Macroeconomic Fluctuations." *Journal of Development Economics* 91 (2): 211–26.

Galeano, L., A. Izquierdo, J. P. Puig, C. A. Vegh, and G. Vuletin. 2021. "Can Automatic Government Spending Be Procyclical?" Working Paper 28521, National Bureau of Economic Research, Cambridge, MA.

Gechert, S. 2015. "What Fiscal Policy Is Most Effective? A Meta-Regression Analysis." *Oxford Economic Papers* 67 (3): 553–80.

Gechert, S., C. Paetz, and P. Villanueva. 2020. "The Macroeconomic Effects of Social Security Contributions and Benefits." *Journal of Monetary Economics* 117: 571–84.

Gentilini, U., M. B. A. Almenfi, P. Dale, R. J. Palacios, H. Natarajan, G. A. Galicia Rabadan, and I. V. Santos. 2020. *Social Protection and Jobs Responses to COVID-19: A Real-Time Review of Country Measures.* COVID Living Paper. Washington, DC: World Bank.

Gonzalez-Rozada, M., and H. Ruffo. 2016. "Optimal Unemployment Benefits in the Presence of Informal Labor Markets." *Labour Economics* 41: 204–27.

Hopenhayn, H. A., and J. P. Nicolini. 1997. "Optimal Unemployment Insurance." *Journal of Political Economy* 105 (2): 412–38.

Ilzetzki, E., and C. A. Végh. 2008. "Procyclical Fiscal Policy in Developing Countries: Truth or Fiction?" Working Paper 14191, National Bureau of Economic Research, Cambridge, MA.

Izquierdo, A., C. Pessino, and G. Vuletin, eds. 2018. *Better Spending for Better Lives: How Latin America and the Caribbean Can Do More with Less.* Washington, DC: Inter-American Development Bank.

Jorda, O. 2005. "Estimation and Inference of Impulse Responses by Local Projections." *American Economic Review* 95 (1): 161–82.

Kaminsky, G. L., C. M. Reinhart, and C. A. Végh. 2004. "When It Rains, It Pours: Procyclical Capital Flows and Macroeconomic Policies." *NBER Macroeconomics Annual* 19: 11–53.

Lusardi, A., D. J. Schneider, and P. Tufano. 2011. *Financially Fragile Households: Evidence and Implications.* Working Paper 17072, National Bureau of Economic Research, Cambridge, MA.

Maloney, W. F. 2004. "Informality Revisited." *World Development* 32 (7): 1159–78.

McKay, A., and R. Reis. 2016. "The Role of Automatic Stabilizers in the US Business Cycle." *Econometrica* 84 (1): 141–94.

Nerlich, C., and J. Schroth. 2018. "The Economic Impact of Population Ageing and Pension Reforms." *Economic Bulletin* (2): 85–109.

Oh, H., and R. Reis. 2012. "Targeted Transfers and the Fiscal Response to the Great Recession." Supplement, *Journal of Monetary Economics* 59: S50–S64.

Panadeiros, M., and C. Pessino. 2018. *Consecuencias fiscales del envejecimiento poblacional: proyecciones agregadas del gasto en salud para 10 países de América Latina.* Washington, DC: Inter-American Development Bank.

Parraga-Rodriguez, S. 2018. "The Dynamic Effects of Public Expenditure Shocks in the United States." *Journal of Macroeconomics* 56: 340–60.

Pennings, S. M. 2020. "Cross-Region Transfers in a Monetary Union: Evidence from the US and Some Implications." Policy Research Working Paper 9244, World Bank, Washington, DC.

Perry, G., O. Arias, H. López, W. Maloney, and L. Servén. 2006. *Poverty Reduction and Growth: Virtuous and Vicious Circles.* Washington, DC: World Bank.

Perry, G., W. Maloney, O. Arias, P. Fajnzylber, A. Mason, J. Saavedra-Chanduvi, and M. Bosch. 2007. *Informalidad: Escape y exclusión*. Washington, DC: International Bank for Reconstruction and Development.

Romer, C. D., and D. H. Romer. 2016. "Transfer Payments and the Macroeconomy: The Effects of Social Security Benefit Increases, 1952–1991." *American Economic Journal: Macroeconomics* 8 (4): 1–42.

Stock, J. H., and M. W. Watson. 2007. "Why Has US Inflation Become Harder to Forecast?" *Journal of Money, Credit and Banking* 39 (s1): 3–33.

Talvi, E., and C. A. Vegh. 2005. "Tax Base Variability and Procyclical Fiscal Policy in Developing Countries." *Journal of Development Economics* 78 (1): 156–90.

World Bank. 2020. *The Cost of Staying Healthy*. LAC Semiannual Report. Washington, DC: World Bank.

4

Something Has to Give: Procyclical Pension Benefits and Public Investment in "Bad Times"

Introduction

So far, we have accounted for procyclical and downwardly rigid public consumption in good times and countercyclical downwardly rigid social transfers in bad times in low- and middle-income countries. From a fiscal sustainability perspective, something has to give. Beyond limited increases to public debt (resulting from imperfect credit market access) and default episodes, two types of public spending bear the brunt of fiscal adjustment: social security, mainly consisting of disability insurance and old-age and survivors insurance benefits, and public investment, both of which tend to be procyclical in bad times. This behavior is radically different from that found in high-income economies, where social security tends to be unrelated to the business cycle (because it depends on structural demographic parameters) or mildly countercyclical, because retirements tend to increase during recessions. Public investment, however, is often used in high-income economies as an effective output stabilizer in bad times, and thus it is typically countercyclical.

Why do low- and middle-income markets cut social security spending and public investment? Because they can (and have to). Both types of spending are discretionary and flexible and are thus the typical candidates to serve the country's adjustment efforts. The lack of automatic stabilizers and the rigid nature of public consumption in bad times eventually crowd out both public investment and social security spending as other structural social spending ratchets up in downturns.

Cutting pensions in bad times delivers an important blow to the fight against poverty because pensioners are typically one of the most vulnerable constituencies in low- and middle-income nations. Meanwhile, cutting public investment in countries with already-low levels of public capital hinders their growth prospects substantially.

Procyclical Social Security

Starting with social security spending, its procyclical behavior in low- and middle-income countries is puzzling for a type of expenditure that is typically included in the automatic spending category and considered acyclical in theory and in practice in high-income economies. On the basis of data from 45 countries (27 low and middle income and 18 high income) for the period 1980–2018, we observe that social security spending represents, by and large, the largest component of automatic spending in the high-income and low- and middle-income countries. Specifically, social security spending represents almost 75 percent of automatic spending in high-income countries and 80 percent in low- and middle-income countries. As a percentage of primary spending, social security accounts for 43 percent and 32.5 percent in high-income and low- and middle-income countries, respectively. It is worth noting that this gap is much smaller than that for unemployment insurance spending.

Figure 4.1 shows the cyclicality of social security spending. The correlation is −0.09 (and statistically barely significant) in high-income countries and 0.13 (and statistically significant) in low- and middle-income countries. Moreover, and based on individual country correlations and statistical significance, we find, in line with these group findings, that (1) only 28 percent of high-income countries follow countercyclical policies (the rest exhibit an acyclical profile) and (2) about 45 percent of low- and middle-income countries follow procyclical policies (the rest show an acyclical profile).

Some interesting mechanisms appear when decomposing social security spending into the number of beneficiaries and the amount received by each beneficiary. Performing a simple univariate variance decomposition analysis, about 12 percent of the variance in social security real spending can, on average, be explained by its cyclical component and 88 percent is driven by its trend. These figures are very close to those obtained for family programs' real spending. When focusing on social security beneficiaries, the share explained by its trend increases to 95 percent. This latter fact holds for both high-income and low- and middle-income countries (96 and 94 percent, respectively). To help put things into perspective, even for the number of family programs and benefits beneficiaries, the share explained by its trend is only 74 percent. The fact that fluctuations in social security beneficiaries are almost entirely explained by its trend reflects the intrinsically structural and rigid nature of beneficiaries entitled to this program, which is mainly driven by slowly moving demographic considerations. It also indicates that cyclical fluctuations in social security real spending are mainly driven by cyclical fluctuations in average social security spending per beneficiary as opposed to cyclical movements in the number of social security beneficiaries

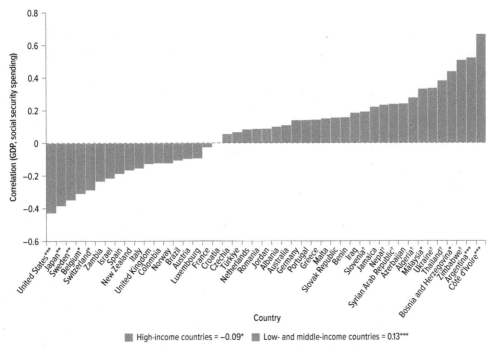

FIGURE 4.1: Country Correlations between the Cyclical Components of Real GDP and Real Social Security Spending

Source: Galeano et al. 2021, based on European System of integrated Social Protection Statistics, Organisation for Economic Co-operation and Development, International Monetary Fund World Economic Outlook database, and national sources.
Note: The cyclical components have been estimated using the Hodrick-Prescott filter. A positive correlation indicates procyclical social security spending; a negative correlation, countercyclical social security spending. Real social security spending is defined as social security spending deflated by the GDP deflator. Correlations are pooled across countries. GDP = gross domestic product.
†p < .15. *p < .10. **p < .05. ***p < .01.

(which are virtually nonexistent). The share of social security real spending per benefi-ciary explained by its trend is 85 percent, which is quite similar to that of real primary spending.

Figure 4.2 shows that, in high-income countries, the barely countercyclical spending behavior observed in figure 4.1 is mainly driven by the countercyclical profile of the number of beneficiaries in some countries (panel a in figure 4.2), as opposed to the behavior observed in the spending per beneficiary, which is acyclical across the board (panel b in figure 4.2). Moreover, as discussed by the World Bank (2009), the number of social security beneficiaries typically increases during a crisis, as people look to early retirement and disability as a means to cope with unemployment. In fact, excluding the years 2009, 2010, and 2011 from the analysis, the number of beneficiaries becomes acyclical (that is, statistically not significant) in each high-income country except Japan.

In sum, although the high-income world shows, by and large, an acyclical social security spending policy profile (as predicted by the theory), and despite the intrinsically structural and rigid nature of this entitlement program (especially regarding the number

FIGURE 4.2: Country Correlations between the Cyclical Components of Real GDP and Real Social Security Spending, by Number of Beneficiaries and Spending per Beneficiary

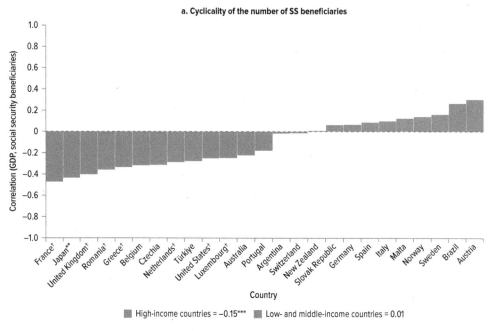

a. Cyclicality of the number of SS beneficiaries

High-income countries = −0.15*** Low- and middle-income countries = 0.01

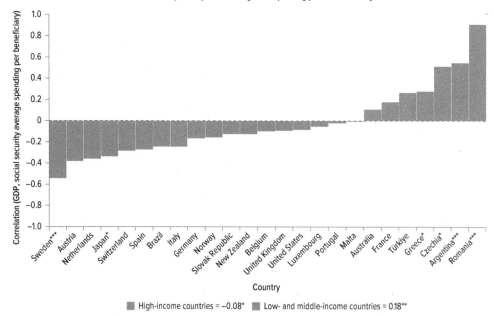

b. Cyclicality of SS average real spending per SS beneficiary

High-income countries = −0.08* Low- and middle-income countries = 0.18**

Source: Galeano et al. 2021, based on European System of integrated Social Protection Statistics, Organisation for Economic Co-operation and Development, International Monetary Fund World Economic Outlook database, and national sources.
Note: The cyclical components have been estimated using the Hodrick-Prescott filter. A positive correlation indicates procyclical social security spending; a negative correlation, countercyclical social security spending. Real SS spending is defined as SS spending deflated by the GDP deflator. Correlations are pooled across countries. GDP = gross domestic product; SS = social security.
†*p* < .15. *p* < .10. **p* < .05. ***p* < .01.

of beneficiaries, which is driven by slowly moving demographic considerations), many low- and middle-income countries show a procyclical social security spending behavior that is essentially driven by fluctuations in individual social security benefit payments. An important question remains: what drives this procyclical behavior?

A key aspect affecting the cyclicality of social security spending in practice is whether adjustments over time of individual social security benefit payments depend on fixed formulas or instead rely more on ad hoc or discretionary decisions by policy makers.

As shown in figure 4.3, on the one hand, high-income countries have historically adjusted individual social security benefit payments following automatic indexation mechanisms, typically linked to changes in the cost of living, such as prices or wages, to maintain retirees' purchasing power constant over time (hereinafter, we use the term *automatic price-based formula indexation mechanism*). On the other hand, fewer than half of low- and middle-income countries have followed automatic price-based formula indexation mechanisms and have instead relied on policy makers' ad hoc or discretionary criteria to adjust individual social security benefit payments. Map 4.1 shows, for the most up-to-date data, whether individual countries in the world rely on automatic price-based formula indexation mechanisms or not.

The lack of automatic price-based formulas seems to be a clear road to procyclicality for social security spending. As figure 4.3 shows, the lower the percentage of years a

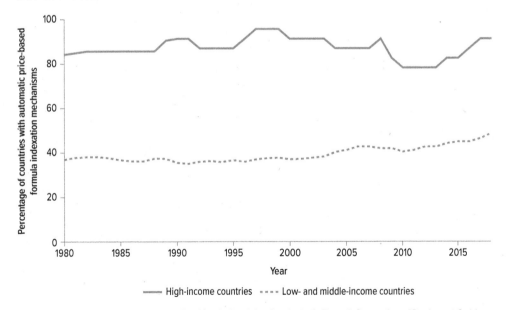

FIGURE 4.3: **Percentage of Countries with Automatic Price-Based Formula Indexation Mechanisms**

Source: Original calculations based on International Social Security Association, Organisation for Economic Co-operation and Development, Social Security Programs Throughout the World data by the U.S. Social Security Administration, and World Bank Pensions Data.
Note: One hundred forty-three countries are included.

Existence of Automatic Price-Based Formula Indexation Mechanisms in the World, circa 2019

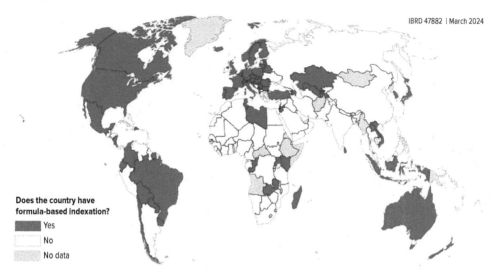

IBRD 47882 | March 2024

Does the country have formula-based indexation?

- Yes
- No
- No data

Source: Data from Galeano et al. 2021.
Note: Countries in white do not have an automatic price-based formula indexation mechanism. Countries in red rely on an automatic price-based formula indexation mechanism.

country relied on automatic price-based formula indexation (that is, the more a country has relied on ad hoc or discretionary decisions by policy makers), the more procyclical is social security spending. But why is this the case?

There are two important parts to this question. First, we need to understand that, when individual social security benefit payments are adjusted on the basis of automatic price-based formula indexation mechanisms, social security spending is acyclical. The reasons are twofold. First, a slowly moving and intrinsically structural and rigid number of social security beneficiaries are entitled to this program (independent of the nature of the adjustment mechanism, because it is driven by demographic considerations). Second, and more crucially, the automatic price-based formula indexation mechanism itself, by design, aims to maintain retirees' purchasing power (and thus the social security spending per beneficiary) constant over time.

Also, although adjustments of individual social security benefit payments based on ad hoc or discretionary criteria do not necessarily imply procyclicality, in practice, the lack of an automatic price-based formula indexation mechanism reflects underlying borrowing constraints and the inability to save. This, in turn, makes social security spending procyclical because it ends up being determined by social security revenues, which are positively associated with economic activity.

The second important element of public spending "forced" to be procyclical in bad times is public investment. The procyclicality of public investment is clearly shown in figure 4.4.

FIGURE 4.4: **Public Investment Is Procyclical**

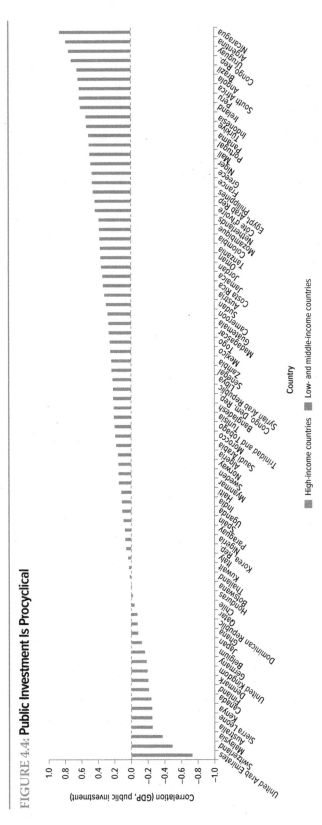

Source: Original calculations based on the International Monetary Fund World Economic Outlook database (2019).

Note: The cyclical components have been estimated using the Hodrick-Prescott filter. A positive correlation indicates procyclical fiscal policy; a negative correlation, countercyclical fiscal policy. Public investment is defined as general government net acquisition of nonfinancial assets deflated by the GDP deflator. Data used in the analysis spans from 1980 to 2019. GDP = gross domestic product.

Why is it easier to cut public investment than public consumption during bad times? As is well known in the political budget cycle literature, politicians tend to bias their spending decisions toward the policies that favor their own voters the most (see Drazen 2000; Franzese and Jusko 2006). The effects of public spending on public goods or public transfers are immediately felt by voters, and thus, we could say that these types of expenditures have an "active constituency." The positive effects of public investment are not noticeable to the public until the medium to long run and so have less political value. This means that it is easier to expand current expenditures and transfers during good times. Similarly, in times of economic adjustment, capital expenditure cuts may prove to be more politically palatable than cuts in current expenditure, because the costs of cutting investment are harder for voters to perceive in bad times.

The opportunity cost of cutting public investment in terms of long-term growth could be sizable. Public investment not only stimulates aggregate demand but can also improve productivity in the private sector, especially in countries with little public infrastructure. Given its importance to long-term growth and the fact that the completion of large infrastructure projects may span beyond the typical business cycle, public investment spending delivers the largest returns when it follows structural needs as opposed to cyclical changes. For countries with already large stocks of public capital, public investment could also be an important tool to reinvigorate employment and private investment during times of economic slack.

Just how big is the contribution of public investment cuts to fiscal adjustments? Figure 4.5 displays the average composition of fiscal adjustments for a sample of 18 countries in Latin America and the Caribbean (LAC) for the period from 1988 to 2017. The figure divides total primary government spending into two components (primary current spending and public investment) and, in turn, primary current spending into

FIGURE 4.5: **Typical Adjustment Spending Composition in Latin America and the Caribbean**

Source: Végh et al. 2018.
Note: Based on a sample of 18 LAC countries for the period 1988–2017 (see Annex 4A for a definition of the LAC countries). All variables are expressed in real terms. High inflation is defined as an inflation rate of at least 10 percent per year. LAC = Latin America and the Caribbean.

two components (public consumption, which includes wages and goods and services, and social transfers). The sample is then divided into two columns representing spending composition relative to total spending during high and low inflation episodes, respectively.

It is clear from figure 4.5 that cuts to public investment receive the brunt of the adjustment. During this period, investment cuts represented 82 percent of the whole adjustment.

This important bias against public investment spending over the cycle means that although the composition of public spending has remained constant in high-income economies since 1990, it has changed dramatically in low- and middle-income economies. Figure 4.6 depicts the evolution of primary spending composition in low- and middle-income economies since 1980. The overall cumulative bias against public investment amounts to an astonishing 4.3 percentage points of total primary spending in the period from 1990 to 2019 alone.

The direct consequences of the bias against public investment in low- and middle-income countries are that large contractions of public sector investment in key infrastructure projects were most needed to consolidate long-run growth. Figure 4.7 showcases how public infrastructure investment in LAC has been falling steadily, from roughly 4 percent in 1980 to 1.3 percent by 2019. Much of the fall in investment over time has been driven by the retrenchment of the public sector from 3 percent of gross domestic product (GDP) to 1 percent, which has not been offset by the moderate increase in private sector investment.

FIGURE 4.6: **Evolution of Public Spending Composition in Low- and Middle-Income Countries as a Percentage of Total Primary Spending**

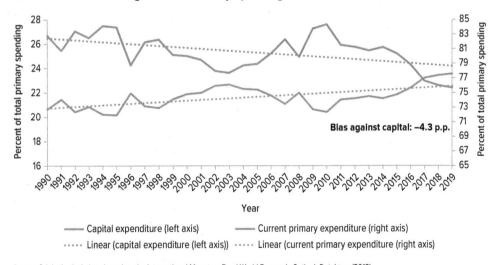

Source: Original calculations based on the International Monetary Fund World Economic Outlook Database (2019).
Note: Real government capital spending is defined as general government net acquisition of nonfinancial assets. Real government current primary spending is defined as general government current spending net of interest payments. Total primary spending is defined as the sum of capital and current primary spending. Variables are deflated by the GDP deflator. The bias is defined by the absolute variation of capital spending share between 1990 and 2019. Refer to Annex 4A for definition of low- and middle-income economies. GDP = gross domestic product; p.p. = percentage point.

FIGURE 4.7: **Infrastructure Investment for Selected Latin American and the Caribbean Countries**

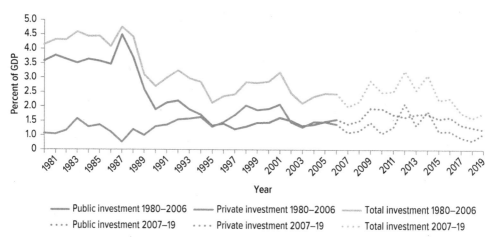

Source: Original elaboration based on data from Calderón and Servén 2010 for 1980–2006, Infralatam for public sector data for 2007–17, and World Bank Private Participation in Infrastructure (PPI) Database for the private sector for 2007 and 2017 (except for Chile, which is not reported in the PPI Database). Includes telecommunications, water, energy, and transport (only roads and railways from 1980 to 2006).
Note: Included countries are Argentina, Brazil, Chile, Colombia, Mexico, and Peru. The values are GDP weighted. GDP = gross domestic product.

Low levels of infrastructure investment since 1990 contributed to the widening infrastructure gap in LAC, which is estimated to be 3.4 percent of GDP in capital and 1.1 percent in maintenance (Rozenberg and Fay 2019). Together, the needed investment would be 2.0 percent in transport, 1.4 percent in energy, 0.7 percent in water and sanitation, 0.3 percent in flood protection, and 0.1 percent in irrigation, which are significantly above current levels. As a longer-term goal, 16 countries in LAC would need to invest at least 2 percentage points over current levels to close the infrastructure gap (Castellani et al. 2019). In the short to medium term, the gap in infrastructure services can be narrowed by ensuring that spending is well targeted and efficient.

To sum up, in good times, low- and middle-income markets increase spending inefficiently in downwardly rigid components of spending. In bad times, the lack of unemployment insurance forces low- and middle-income markets to increase downwardly rigid transfers. This procyclical rigid behavior in good times and countercyclical rigid behavior in bad times creates serious sustainability problems. Some of this is compensated for with lower pensions, but it is mostly adjusted through public investment, which creates additional problems in the long run.

The Wrong Solution to an Unnecessary Problem

As described in chapter 2, procyclical behaviors in good times and countercyclical transfers in bad times lead to fiscal unsustainability; something has to give. Political economy arguments and weak institutions lead to procyclical behavior of public investment and social security transfers during bad times. Although the procyclicality of these spending components may relieve some of the fiscal pressure experienced by low- and middle-income markets in bad times, these compositional biases may represent an important drag on long-term growth for these economies. In this section, we try to quantify the consequences of cuts to public investment and social security for economic performance, thus estimating the effective cost of being resilient for low- and middle-income markets.

Cutting Public Investment Is Especially Costly for Low- and Middle-Income Markets

Contrary to the typically small public consumption multipliers, early theoretical work by Aschauer (1989a, 1989b) and Baxter and King (1993) and more recent empirical evidence (for example, Auerbach and Gorodnichenko 2013; Calderón, Moral-Benito, and Servén 2015; Eden and Kraay 2014; Furceri and Li 2017; Leduc and Wilson 2013) have found that the public investment multiplier can be quite large. Beyond the direct Keynesian effect on aggregate demand, which is shared with government consumption, these large multipliers can be explained through a supply-side effect in which public investment directly improves the economy's productive capacity by increasing the marginal product of private capital and labor. As time progresses, this generates positive effects on both private investment and private consumption.

Public investment plays a very important role in the efforts of low- and middle-income markets to raise economic growth, increase productivity, and reinvigorate the role of the private sector.

Although public investment in low- and middle-income markets is afflicted by efficiency issues such as cost overruns, implementation delays, institutional weaknesses, and wasteful use of resources (including corruption), Izquierdo et al. (2019) find that the size of their multiplier can still be very large because of low- and middle-income markets' low levels of initial capital stock.

The link between the initial stock of capital and the returns to an additional unit of investment is straightforward. Standard neoclassical fiscal policy growth models (such as the classic contribution of Baxter and King 1993) would predict that the lower the initial stock of public capital is, the larger the output effects of increasing public investment.

Specifically, when the initial stock of public capital is low, the marginal productivity of an additional unit of public investment is large, which, aided also by additional private investment, will lead to higher public investment multipliers. Conversely, when the initial stock of public capital is high, the impact of additional public investment should be low. Hence, in the case of low- and middle-income countries (low stock of public capital), public investment multipliers should be higher.

Izquierdo et al. (2019) provide empirical evidence that low stocks of initial capital in low- and middle-income markets are largely responsible for the large public investment multipliers observed in low- and middle-income nations. This result holds even when we take into account the large inefficiencies associated with public investment in these countries. Izquierdo et al. (2019) obtain empirical evidence of this link from different methodologies and data samples.

Using quarterly data for a large set of European nations divided by high-income economies in the west and low- and middle-income countries in the east, Izquierdo et al. (2019) exploit large differences in the initial stock of capital for these countries to test their link to public investment multipliers. Figure 4.8 shows the sample of countries used in the study and their levels of stock of public capital relative to GDP in 1990 (starting period). These levels differ significantly and go from 180 percent of GDP in Denmark to barely 18 percent in Hungary.

Using the impulse responses to a US$1 increase in public investment showcased in figure 4.9, we can see that the size of the initial stock of public capital matters. Panels a, b, and c show the multipliers associated with a public investment shock evaluated at the high ratio (95th percentile of the sample, or 1.33 ratio) on GDP, private consumption, and private investment, respectively. Panels d, e, and f show the same multipliers but are evaluated at the low ratio (5th percentile of the sample, or 0.16 ratio). On impact, the multipliers are quite similar (and small) regardless of the ratio of the initial stock of public capital to GDP (0.25 in panel a and 0.18 in panel d).

As the horizon becomes larger, however, the difference between the two multipliers grows markedly. For the case of the high ratio, the size of the multiplier remains small and statistically weak, reaching 0.15 ($t = 0.2$) after two years of the public investment shock. In sharp contrast, when starting with a low ratio, the multiplier becomes larger with a longer time horizon, reaching 2.15 ($t = 2.1$) after two years of the public

FIGURE 4.8: **Ratio of the Initial Stock of Public Capital to GDP in European Countries**

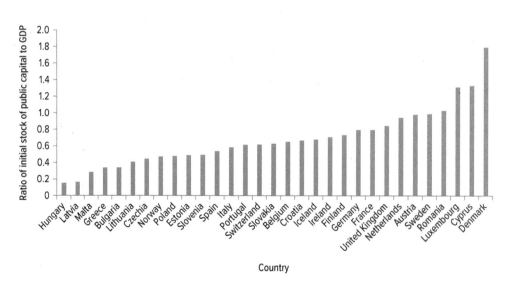

Source: Izquierdo et al. 2019.
Note: GDP = gross domestic product.

PUBLIC SPENDING POLICIES IN LATIN AMERICA AND THE CARIBBEAN

Public Investment Multiplier: Evidence from European Countries

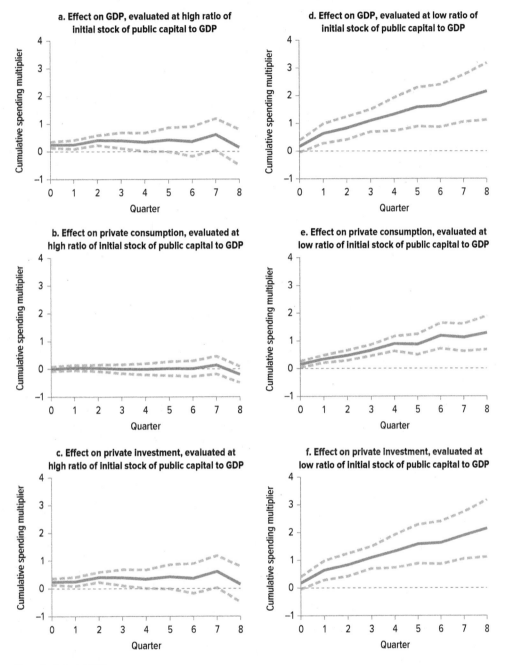

Source: Izquierdo et al. 2019.

Note: Country fixed-effect panel regression with linear and quadratic trends; standard errors are Driscoll–Kraay (1998) standard errors and bootstrapped. Evaluated at high (95th percentile) and low (5th percentile) ratios of the initial stock of public capital over GDP ratios. GDP = gross domestic product.

investment shock. We cannot reject the null hypothesis that this multiplier is larger than one, statistically speaking. This reflects the stronger response of both private consumption (panel e) and private investment (panel f).

Focusing on the effect after two years of the public investment shock, figure 4.10 illustrates the crucial role played by the ratio of the initial stock of public capital to GDP on the size of the public investment multiplier by plotting the latter as a function of the former. Although the multiplier is statistically zero at high levels of the ratio of the initial stock of public capital to GDP (that is, higher than 1.00), it becomes statistically significant and increasingly positive with lower ratios. Moreover, for sufficiently low levels of the ratio (that is, lower than 0.25), the public investment multiplier becomes larger than one. In other words, the increase or fall of GDP associated with, respectively, increasing or reducing public investment by US$1 tends to be zero for high levels of the ratio of the initial stock of public capital to GDP and becomes larger as the initial ratio decreases.

These findings have important policy implications given that the ratio of the initial stock of public capital to GDP varies greatly across countries (and over time) and thus so will the size of the public investment multipliers. As an illustration, map 4.2 shows the implied public investment multipliers for our European sample for the ratio of the initial stock of public capital to GDP prevailing in 1990 (panel a) and 2014 (panel b). Interestingly, between 1990 and 2014, the public investment multiplier fell the most in southern economies and among new members from the eastern bloc. This came about because of important rises in the stock of public capital, following efforts to increase the stock of infrastructure and other productive investments in least-favored regions as a result of the European Regional Development Fund and the Cohesion Fund.

FIGURE 4.10: **Public Investment Multiplier after Two Years of the Spending Shock, Evaluated at Different Ratios of the Initial Stock of Public Capital to GDP: Evidence from European Countries**

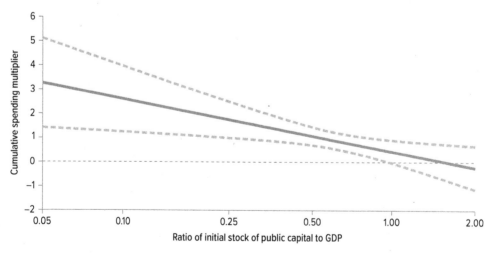

Source: Izquierdo et al. 2019.
Note: Country fixed-effect panel regression with linear and quadratic trends; standard errors are Driscoll-Kraay standard errors and bootstrapped. GDP = gross domestic product.

MAP 4.2: Evolution of Public Investment Multipliers in Europe

a. Evaluated in 1990

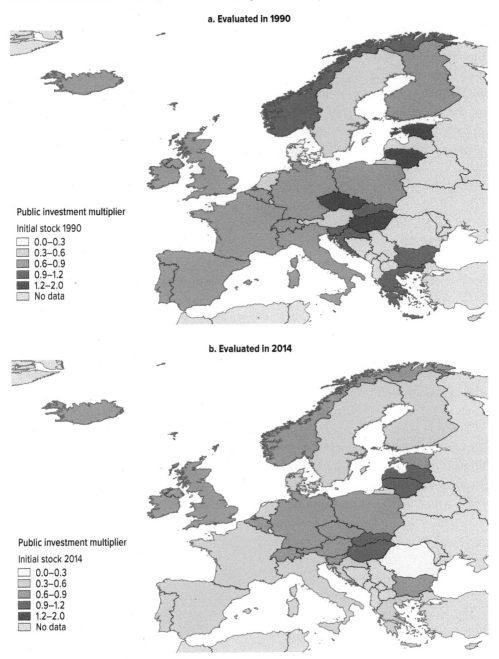

Public investment multiplier

Initial stock 1990

- 0.0–0.3
- 0.3–0.6
- 0.6–0.9
- 0.9–1.2
- 1.2–2.0
- No data

b. Evaluated in 2014

Public investment multiplier

Initial stock 2014

- 0.0–0.3
- 0.3–0.6
- 0.6–0.9
- 0.9–1.2
- 1.2–2.0
- No data

Source: Izquierdo et al. 2019.

Using the stock of paved highways as a proxy for public investment, Izquierdo et al. (2019) present further evidence of the link between the initial stock of public capital and the public investment multipliers for the 23 Argentine provinces during the period 1964–2014.

Figure 4.11 shows that the public investment multiplier associated with the proxy for a high initial stock of public capital over GDP, 0.23, is much smaller than that associated with the proxy for a low initial stock of public capital over GDP, 2.03. In fact, we can say that the former multiplier is statistically zero, and the latter multiplier is larger than one. As with the European sample, these results show the crucial effect of the initial stock of public capital over GDP on the size of the provincial public investment multiplier.[1] Evaluating these results two years after the shock, the multiplier is virtually zero for high levels of this ratio (that is, higher than 1.20), and it becomes statistically significant and increasingly positive with lower initial ratios. Moreover, for sufficiently low levels of this ratio (that is, lower than 0.30), the public investment multiplier becomes larger than one. In other words, the increase or fall of GDP associated with, respectively, increasing or reducing provincial public investment by US$1 tends to be zero for high levels of the initial stock of public capital over GDP in each province and becomes larger as the initial ratio decreases.

These findings have important policy implications given that our proxy for the ratio of initial stock of public capital over GDP varies greatly across Argentine provinces (and over time) and, thus, so will the size of the public investment multipliers.

Map 4.3 shows the implied public investment multipliers for Argentine provinces given our proxy for the ratio of stock of public capital over GDP in, for example, the years 1964 (panel a), 1990 (panel b), and 2014 (panel c).

Of concern for its long-run development, the province of Buenos Aires (which accounts for about 40 percent of Argentina's GDP and has increased its GDP almost threefold since 1964) has barely increased its stock of paved highways (with less than a 10 percent increase from 4,300 kilometers in 1964 to about 4,700 kilometers in 2014). For this reason, its public investment multiplier almost doubled from 0.80 in 1964 to 1.50 in 2014. In contrast, other provinces, including the province of La Rioja, have increased their stock of paved highways by about fivefold, from 392 kilometers in 1964 to about 1,900 kilometers in 2014. As a result, its public investment multiplier fell from 1.62 in 1964 to virtually zero in 2014.

Finally, extrapolating estimates from Izquierdo et al. (2019) for a global sample, map 4.4 shows the relatively big impact in the medium- to long-term economic growth compositional changes in public spending away from public investment in low- and middle-income markets. Although on-impact effects may be relatively small, every forgone dollar in public investment may lead to a large and long-lasting negative impact on long-term economic growth.

FIGURE 4.11: Primary Spending and Public Investment Multipliers: Evidence from Argentine Provinces

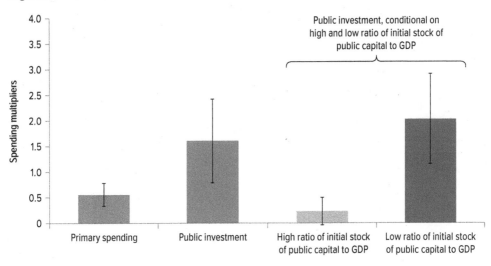

Source: Izquierdo et al. 2019.
Note: The 5th percentile and 95th percentile are used to identify the low and high ratio, respectively, of the initial stock of public capital to GDP in Argentine provinces. Provincial fixed-effect panel regression with linear and quadratic trends; standard errors are Driscoll-Kraay (1998) standard errors and bootstrapped. GDP = gross domestic product.

MAP 4.3: Evolution of the Investment Multipliers for Argentine Provinces

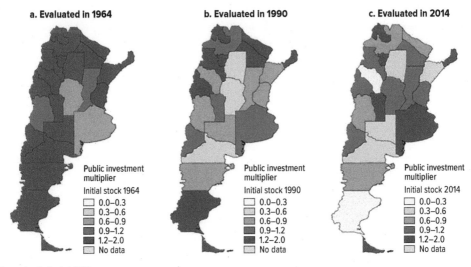

Source: Izquierdo et al. 2019.

MAP 4.4: Global Extrapolation of Public Investment Multipliers Based on Initial Stock

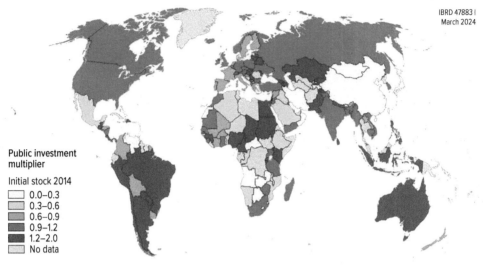

IBRD 47883 |
March 2024

Public investment multiplier

Initial stock 2014
- ☐ 0.0–0.3
- ☐ 0.3–0.6
- ☐ 0.6–0.9
- ☐ 0.9–1.2
- ☐ 1.2–2.0
- ☐ No data

Source: Izquierdo et al. 2019.

Annex 4A: Categorization of Countries

TABLE 4A.1: Categorization of Countries in Chapter 4 Figures

Figure	Category	Countries Included
Figure 4.5	LAC countries	Argentina, Brazil, Bolivia, Chile, Colombia, Costa Rica, Dominican Republic, Ecuador, El Salvador, Guatemala, Haiti, Honduras, Mexico, Nicaragua, Panama, Paraguay, Peru, and Uruguay
Figure 4.6	Low- and middle-income economies	Algeria, Bahamas, the; Bahrain; Bangladesh, Benin, Brunei Darussalam, Burkina Faso; Central African Republic; Chile, Comoros; Congo, Rep.; Costa Rica; Djibouti; Dominica; Eswatini; Equatorial Guinea; Ethiopia; Gabon; Ghana; Guinea; Honduras; Iceland; Jamaica; Jordan; Kuwait; Lesotho; Malaysia; Maldives; Mexico; Morocco; Mozambique; Oman; Paraguay; Philippines; Saudi Arabia; Seychelles; St. Lucia; St. Vincent and Grenadines; Sudan; Suriname; Togo; Trinidad and Tobago; Yemen, Rep.

Note: LAC = Latin America and the Caribbean.

Note

1. Although our results show that, holding all else constant, the returns to public investment will be larger whenever the initial level of capital is smaller, there may be other important determinants of these multipliers, including the availability of complementary factors (see, for example, Grover, Lall, and Maloney 2022).

References

Ardanaz, M., and A. Izquierdo. 2017. "Current Expenditure Upswings in Good Times and Public Investment Downswings in Bad Times? New Evidence from Developing Countries." *Journal of Comparative Economics* 50 (1): 118–34.

Aschauer, D. A. 1989a. "Does Public Capital Crowd out Private Capital?" *Journal of Monetary Economics* 24 (2): 171–88.

Aschauer, D. A. 1989b. "Is Public Expenditure Productive?" *Journal of Monetary Economics* 23 (2): 177–200.

Auerbach, A. J., and Y. Gorodnichenko. 2013. "Output Spillovers from Fiscal Policy." *American Economic Review* 103 (3): 141–6.

Baxter, M., and R. G. King. 1993. "Fiscal Policy in General Equilibrium." *American Economic Review* 83 (3): 315–34.

Calderón, C., E. Moral-Benito, and L. Servén. 2015. "Is Infrastructure Capital Productive? A Dynamic Heterogeneous Approach." *Journal of Applied Econometrics* 30 (2): 177–98.

Calderón, C., and L. Servén. 2010. "Infrastructure in Latin America." Policy Research Working Paper 5317, World Bank, Washington, DC.

Castellani, F., M. Olarreaga, U. Panizza, and Y. Zhou. 2019. "Investment Gaps in Latin America and the Caribbean." *International Development Policy* 11.1.

Drazen, A. 2000. *Political Economy in Macroeconomics*. Princeton, NJ: Princeton University Press.

Driscoll, J. C., and A. C. Kraay. 1998. "Consistent Covariance Matrix Estimation with Spatially Dependent Panel Data." *Review of Economics and Statistics* 80 (4): 549–60.

Eden, M., and A. Kraay. 2014. "'Crowding In' and the Returns to Government Investment in Low-Income Countries." Policy Research Working Paper WPS6781, World Bank, Washington, DC.

Franzese, R., and K. L. Jusko. 2006. "Political-Economic Cycles." In *Oxford Handbook of Political Economy*, edited by B. R. Weingast and D. A. Wittman, 545–64. Oxford: Oxford University Press.

Furceri, D., and B. G. Li. 2017. "The Macroeconomic (and Distributional) Effects of Public Investment in Developing Economies." Working Paper WP/17/217, International Monetary Fund, Washington, DC.

Galeano, L., A. Izquierdo, J. P. Puig, C. A. Vegh, and G. Vuletin. 2021. "Can Automatic Government Spending Be Procyclical?" Working Paper 28521, National Bureau of Economic Research, Cambridge, MA.

Grover, A., S. Lall, and W. Maloney. 2022. *Place, Productivity, and Prosperity: Revisiting Spatially Targeted Policies for Regional Development*. Washington, DC: World Bank.

Izquierdo, A., R. E. Lama, J. P. Medina, J. P. Puig, D. Riera-Crichton, C. A. Vegh, and G. Vuletin. 2019. "Is the Public Investment Multiplier Higher in Developing Countries? An Empirical Investigation." Working Paper WP/19/289, International Monetary Fund, Washington, DC.

Leduc, S., and D. Wilson. 2013. "Roads to Prosperity or Bridges to Nowhere? Theory and Evidence on the Impact of Public Infrastructure Investment." *NBER Macroeconomics Annual* 27 (1): 89–142.

Rozenberg, J., and M. Fay, eds. 2019. *Beyond the Gap: How Countries Can Afford the Infrastructure They Need While Protecting the Planet*. Washington, DC: World Bank.

Végh, C. A., G. Vuletin, D. Riera-Crichton, D. Friedheim, L. Morano, and J. A. Camarena. 2018. *Fiscal Adjustment in Latin America and the Caribbean: Short-Run Pain, Long-Run Gain?* Washington, DC: World Bank.

World Bank. 2009. *Pensions in Crisis: Europe and Central Asia Regional Policy Note*. Report No. 58460. Washington, DC: World Bank.

5
Conclusion and Policy Prescriptions

Political economy considerations related to the common pool problem (that is, the tendency for politicians to exploit limited resources to capture benefits that would otherwise go to opposing parties), voters' fiscal illusion, and policy makers' short-termism push low- and middle-income countries to deliver inefficient, unsustainable, and procyclical fiscal policies. Legislated fiscal rules can help mitigate these issues by constraining the use of discretionary spending as long as they are applied effectively and monitored by an independent, well-informed institution. However, aggregate rules—that is, those applied to overall primary spending—may lead to harmful compositional effects. Going beyond "big G," this report shows that not all spending is the same, and it is critical to unpack the subcomponents. Procyclical, downwardly rigid, and inefficient public consumption during good times coupled with ratcheting up of transfer programs that stand in for absent automatic stabilizers lead to unsustainable fiscal paths. Moreover, correcting for these deficits typically involves cutting public investment and pensions, which leads to long-term welfare losses. Hence, better understanding of the cyclicality and rigidities associated with each component of public spending can help policy makers set up the right institutional framework to contain procyclicality, protect social spending, and avoid growth-deterring compositional shifts. In particular, our study shows the importance of containing rigid spending on both sides of the business cycle in favor of retractable spending that can be used in the design of counter-cyclical policies.

In the following sections, we highlight several policy tools that address each one of the fiscal policy anomalies described in previous chapters. Although not an exhaustive list, we discuss expenditure rules (ERs), better design of transfer programs, investment-friendly fiscal rules, rules for protecting pension obligations, and the use of the cyclical squeeze as an impetus for increased government efficiency.

Dealing with Procyclical, Inefficient, and Downwardly Rigid Public Consumption: From a Butcher's Knife to a Surgeon's Scalpel

Public consumption in low- and middle-income markets is inefficient, procyclical, and downwardly rigid, which limits fiscal space and hence the potential for countercyclical policy in downturns. Because inefficiency, procyclicality, and spending rigidities are rooted in countries' political economy and weak institutions, the typical policy prescription addresses the need to improve the quality of those political and fiscal bodies.

In an effort to address issues of fiscal sustainability, policy makers around the world have favored the introduction of fiscal rules (as of 2021, about 105 economies have adopted at least one fiscal rule). These rules are long-term constraints on fiscal policy through numerical limits on the budgetary aggregates. Not only does a fiscal rule limit political decisions made by the executive, but it can also be used to assess the executive's management of fiscal policy. The most common types of fiscal rules are balanced budget rules (BBRs) and debt rules (DRs). The former are constitutional or statutory rules that prohibit states from spending more than they collect in revenue. The latter establishes debt limits according to the government's repayment capacity (i.e., the ratio between debt service and revenues). Several major crises, including the financial collapse of 2008 and the commodity slowdown five years later, have forced important revisions in the design of fiscal rules to increase their effectiveness and compliance. Among these upgrades we find (1) escape clauses, which were an essential feature of the stronger legal basis of "second-generation" fiscal rules (Eyraud et al. 2018), with rules added to constitutions in several instances; (2) improvements in formal enforcement by adding the fiscal rules in annual budget preparations and medium-term fiscal frameworks, thus increasing the accountability of the government for *ex post* compliance; and (3) increased focus on stabilization by making the rules sensitive to fluctuations over business cycles. During this evolution of fiscal rules, tensions among simplicity, enforceability, and effectiveness arise when deciding between the number and type of rules that need to be applied. Simple BBRs are easier to implement and enforce but typically lead to procyclical policies (Alesina and Bayouni 1996; Clemens and Miran 2012; Fatás and Mihov 2006). Structural budget rules targeting the fiscal position after controlling for the estimated budgetary consequences of the business cycle address the cyclicality problem but require an objective evaluation of macroeconomic factors by an independent and capable fiscal council.[1] In fact, recent efforts to increase the reputational costs of noncompliance underscore the importance of this independent fiscal institution (International Monetary Fund 2013). Although these nonpartisan bodies represent a new innovation in low- and middle-income markets and outside the European Union, they could play a crucial role as public finance watchdogs, enhancing fiscal policy credibility and performing tasks such as overseeing rule compliance and validating macroeconomic and fiscal forecasts. A large number of individual spending rules may be difficult to track and could cause unintended compositional effects (Blanchard and Giavazzi 2004).

Responding to high economic volatility during the late 1990s and early 2000s, the adoption of fiscal rules in Latin America and the Caribbean (LAC) has been a gradual and varied process across countries. Valencia and Ulloa-Suarez (2022) show that as of 2022, Argentina, The Bahamas, Barbados, Brazil, Chile, Colombia, Costa Rica, Ecuador, El Salvador, Honduras, Jamaica, Mexico, Panama, Paraguay, Peru, and Uruguay had adopted at least one fiscal rule. These countries overwhelmingly chose to implement a broad BBR, although, recognizing the need to address procyclical biases, two-thirds of them adopted more than one rule. The most common rule combinations were an ER and a fiscal balance rule, adopted by four countries, and a fiscal balance rule and a DR, adopted by three countries. In addition, as of 2021, Brazil, Chile, Colombia, Costa Rica, Grenada, Mexico, Panama, Peru, and Uruguay had established fiscal councils to monitor their fiscal rules. These institutions vary in their operational role and independence from the political fiscal authority. For example, Chile's Autonomous Fiscal Council reports its findings to Parliament in a formal hearing as part of the yearly budget process and enjoys both legal and operational independence. In contrast, Colombia's Comité Consultivo Para la Regla Fiscal has no role in the budget process and lacks operational independence (see Davoodi et al. 2022).

Finding the Right Amount of Rigidity

Although balanced budget fiscal rules impose fiscal policy rigidities by (symmetrically) constraining the execution of fiscal rules on both sides of the business cycle, it is important to note that not all rigidities are the same. Downward rigidity of public consumption is a characteristic that low- and middle-income markets share with high-income economies. Some degree of rigidity is desirable: society may not want governments to cut basic public services such as education, health, or safety every time the economy hits turbulence. However, the documented upward ratcheting of spending and contraction of fiscal space suggests excess rigidity. Governments in low- and middle-income markets can still lessen inefficient budget rigidities by, for example, providing better medium-term fiscal planning directed by an independent government budget office so that only the necessary spending is tied up; enhancing transparency throughout the budgeting process; reducing budget fragmentation, thus allowing for a more expedient budget approval process; and limiting earmarking throughout the budgeting process.[2] In the LAC region, only Chile and Uruguay have independent fiscal institutions that actively participate in the congressional budget process.

Outside of inefficiencies in the budgeting process that create excess rigidities in downturns, the main difference between low- and middle-income markets and high-income economies when managing public consumption lays in the actions taken during upturns. High-income economies tend to spend moderately, following structural income trends and, thus, generating fiscal savings that can be applied during downturns. This effectively renders public consumption in high-income economies acyclical.

Expenditure Rules: The Surgeon's Scalpel

The lesson of this report is that although a well-designed and implemented BBR could help address sustainability concerns, it may prove too broad to address the original sin in our story, that is, unsustainable increases in public spending during good times. Switching from the butcher's knife to a surgeon's scalpel has been attempted by using ERs that could apply to a wide set of spending subcategories. ERs typically take the form of a cap on nominal or real spending growth over the medium term. Unlike the deficit caps imposed by general BBRs, where governments spend most of the revenue windfalls as political pressures become difficult to resist, by presetting the maximum level of spending, ERs automatically create fiscal space as soon as high revenue growth becomes binding.

ERs are also more transparent and easier to monitor, and they tend to have a better compliance record because they are directly related to the formulation of the annual budget, which sets legally binding appropriations (Ayuso-i-Casals 2012). With BBRs, ERs need well-defined escape clauses with clear implementation protocols to be effective. Several countries in LAC, including Argentina, Brazil, Colombia, and Peru, have ERs currently in place. Among these countries, only Brazil has an independent active monitoring agency for compliance and formal enforcement procedure.

Fiscal Rules in Practice

Recent studies have shown that fiscal rules enhance debt sustainability by improving fiscal balances and reducing fiscal policy procyclicality. The positive impacts depend heavily on the degree of compliance with the rules (see Bouwen 2009; Debrun et al. 2008, 2013; Fall et al. 2015; Heinemann and Yeter 2018; Iara and Wolff 2014; Marneffe et al. 2011; and Wyplosz 2013, among others).

Among low- and middle-income markets, Chile, with a well-implemented and closely monitored structural BBR since the early 2000s, has been the poster child for success in delivering effective and sustainable countercyclical fiscal policies. The effectiveness of this rule relies heavily on the way the rule is designed and the ability of government to enforce it. In the Chilean case, the design of the balanced structural deficit mandate allows room for countercyclical policies. At the same time, Chile has an independent body of fiscal experts providing key inputs and monitoring implementation of the rule. Chile's use of a stabilization fund created on copper earnings helped provide extra public savings in a time of need.[3] In a global sample, the presence of BBRs has a positive but statistically insignificant effect on fiscal balances, but this effect becomes significant among countries that comply with them. Countries that comply with their BBRs also exhibit a statistically significant reduction in debt levels and an increase in the responsiveness of the primary balance to changes in the debt stock.

Compliance with all fiscal rules in LAC fell sharply after the 2008 financial crisis, during the commodity price crash in the years following, and in the aftermath of the COVID-19 pandemic. Structural rules and DRs have had the highest compliance rates, and ERs have had the lowest (Valencia and Ulloa-Suarez 2022). The design of the rules has a significant impact on compliance rates. Clear procedures for implementation and enforcement, including automatic correction mechanisms, predetermined consequences for noncompliance, and clearly defined authority to take corrective action, jointly with sensible escape clauses, help increase compliance rates.

Although these rules are now common among low- and middle-income markets and present in most LAC countries,[4] poorly defined escape clauses allow countries to move away from the rules during bad times, adding moral hazard to their spending in good times and downward rigidity during bad times. As discussed in box 5.1, Peru's experience with BBRs in the past decade offers a guide to both good and bad practices.

With a more targeted and simplistic approach, ERs are also associated with more spending control, countercyclical fiscal policy, and improved fiscal discipline (see Cordes et al. 2015). ERs are particularly effective in reducing expenditure procyclicality. When combined with fiscal councils or sovereign wealth funds, ERs can reduce expenditure procyclicality by as much as 40 percent (Blanco et al. 2020). ERs tend to be simpler to implement and more transparent, and they contain fewer technical requirements.

BOX 5.1: Peru's Recent Experience with Budget Balance Rules

In October 2013, Peru replaced its budget balance rule (BBR) with mandated ex ante guidelines for the structural balance of the nonfinancial public sector (NFPS). In this strengthened framework, a new government must enact a macrofiscal policy statement within 90 days of assuming office that details the guidelines for the structural balance of the NFPS for the whole presidential period. After correcting for the budgetary effects of the business cycle, the deficit cannot not exceed 1 percent of gross domestic product (GDP). Peru also established clear operational guidance and independent monitoring on the activation of the escape clause in the event of a natural disaster or international crisis.

In August 2015, Peru invoked its escape clause and increased the deficit target from 1 to 3 percent of GDP as a result of the El Niño natural disaster and the fall in international commodity prices. For this case, Peruvian Fiscal Responsibility Law 30099 clearly defined the procedural mechanisms. First, the Finance Ministry would present a report no longer than five calendar days after a national emergency was declared requiring the approval of the Council of Ministers. Once submitted to Congress, the new bill had to include a set of proposals to mitigate the natural disaster or national emergency, new expenditure targets of the NFPS for the next three years, a detailed account of how to return to the previous fiscal targets, and fiscal adjustments for the regional and local governments. Once the bill was prepared, the Peruvian Fiscal Council had to provide a recommendation on the proposal within five calendar days. This mechanism ensured the availability of resources in the short run to address the crisis and also the return to a sustainable path in the medium run.

In contrast to the actions taken in 2015, facing COVID-19 in 2020, Peruvian authorities did not use their escape clause and decided instead to enact new legislation to bypass the fiscal rule altogether. Presumably, the formal escape route would have included conditions for fiscal recovery measures postsuspension. Bypassing the rule provided resources to address the pandemic but not a clear path to recover fiscal sustainability.

ERs are most effective in improving debt sustainability when combined with DRs or BBRs. Although ERs are expected to exhibit high compliance rates because of their ease of implementation and monitoring, in LAC these rates have been relatively poor. Low compliance highlights the need to enhance rule design in the region by improving spending flexibility and reconsidering variables such as inflation or GDP for defining spending ceilings.

Although the right combination of fiscal rules can significantly improve the semiprocyclicality of public consumption, they still limit the public sector reaction to economic shocks, especially if those are large and unexpected, such as the COVID-19 pandemic. These constraints may translate into the overcompression of public investment during fiscal retrenchments.

Toward Better-Designed Shock Absorbers: Finding Flexible Alternatives to Unemployment Insurance

Lack of effective automatic stabilizers forces policy makers in low- and middle-income markets to use downwardly rigid social benefits to help improve social conditions during economic downturns. As with the semiprocyclicality of public consumption in good times, the semicountercyclicality of social transfers in bad times leads to fiscal sustainability concerns.

The original sin in this story is the lack of automatic stabilizers, mainly because of the absence, or negligible coverage, of shock absorbers such as unemployment insurance (UI). Of course, a first–best policy prescription would be to improve the deployment of UI, but this is infeasible in economies with large shares of the workforce in informality. It is extremely difficult for countries to control the abuse of unemployment benefits under the cover of informality. For instance, under the typical UI schemes found in high-income economies, if individuals in Mexico were allowed to claim unemployment benefits whenever they were not formally working, more than half of the labor force would qualify. Because a large share of these workers would already be working in the informal sector, receiving these benefits would make this sector even more attractive. Moreover, generous benefits will further incentivize informality (Espino and Sanchez 2013).

Although low- and middle-income countries will eventually establish better automatic stabilizers, in the meantime more attention needs to be directed to improving the design of social transfers, especially if they are going to be actively used as shock absorbers.

Downward rigidity of traditional social transfers in good times is not, in itself, an undesirable social outcome because, theoretically, the lion's share of this expenditure is destined to help mitigate structural social problems. In other words, structural social programs targeting long-run issues such as extreme poverty should be unrelated to short-term economic conditions and may thus appear rigid in upturns. However, these programs have in many cases been retrofitted to serve as cyclical safety nets as well. The difficulty for policy makers is, first, to distinguish the cyclical component of these transfers and, second, to refute the usual political economy arguments that prevent the appropriate retrenchment during the subsequent upturns and ultimately augment the ratcheting effect of social transfers during crises.

Conditional cash transfers (CCTs), which have spread widely in LAC since they were pioneered by Brazil and Mexico in the late 1990s, provide a good example of a structurally designed social program that has been adjusted to attend to cyclical fluctuations in social conditions. CCTs were originally targeted to poor households, and their insistence on children's attendance at school and meeting preventive health goals means they can be considered investments in long-term human capital. The idea was to combine a poverty reduction goal with increases in human capital, both structural and long-term targets. Nonetheless, the ability to quickly deploy and scale the size of existing CCTs makes them an attractive instrument to guard those who are most vulnerable against cyclical macroeconomic shocks. Thus, the programs have steadily expanded through the incorporation of new beneficiaries, and the lack of graduation policies prevented the exit of those who were no longer poor. As a consequence of increased coverage, leakage to nonpoor beneficiaries has been growing. Although CCTs have been an effective tool for redistributing income to poor individuals and expanding beneficiary household members' level of education, and incidence of formal employment and access to basic infrastructure have all increased over time, the overexpansion of the programs beyond those who are chronically poor and their rigid nature have been increasing the pressure on fiscal budgets.

If existing transfers are to also be used as crisis safety nets, introducing several features could reduce their ratchet effect. Generally, policy makers should provide clear guidelines for graduation that foster the exit of those who no longer need social assistance. This would help retrench social spending during expansions as employment recovers and would improve the quality of targeting in these programs. In the case of economic crisis, policy makers could clearly distinguish at inception that, although the crisis transfers use the same mechanisms for distribution, they are fundamentally a different program that will be phased out, thereby clearly delineating the cyclical from structural missions. An even more flexible alternative to scaling up existing social programs could be the provision of emergency transfers that are designed around a limited number of payments linked to the temporal emergency.

LAC economies offered a good example of these practices during the COVID-19 crisis. Brazil, for example, established Auxílio Emergencial (AE), a complement to the existing Bolsa Família. AE was "one of the fastest, most robust, and long-lasting emergency social protection programs offered in developing countries" (World Bank 2021a, 19), with coverage of up to 55.6 percent of the population, considering direct and indirect beneficiaries. The quick organization and implementation of the pandemic emergency assistance were made possible by the infrastructure and databases already in place in Brazil and used for the Bolsa Família program, which has been running since 2003. More important, although the initiative was large (it absorbed 87 percent of total deployed emergency assistance in Brazil, which was up to almost 5 percent of GDP;

Defensoria Pública da União 2021), it was temporary in nature, with unconditional income transfers expected to end by November 2020. Similar efforts were put forward in Argentina (Ingreso Familiar de Emergencia, or IFE), Bolivia (Covid-Bono Familia), Chile (Ingreso Familiar de Emergencia), Costa Rica (Covid-Bono Proteger), Ecuador (Covid—Bono Protection Familiar), Paraguay (Covid-Tekopora), and Peru (Bono Familiar Universal), among other initiatives.

Although by most accounts these extraordinary public efforts were successful in containing the devastating effects of the pandemic among those who were most vulnerable, their intended flexibility and limited time scope waned as the time to retrench neared. In Brazil, the original AE was extended two times before becoming permanent in the shape of a new program, Auxílio Brasil, in 2022. This measure was criticized by opposition parties, with the additional spending being associated with the political cycle as Brazil underwent a general election in 2022. In Argentina, the IFE, a noncontributory benefit of an exceptional nature, delivered five distinct payments to different vulnerable constituencies during the pandemic before migrating to a series of new programs with no clear temporal limit. Ingreso Solidario in Colombia, which was implemented to respond to the social effects of the pandemic in 2020, has reached more than 4 million households so far; it is expected to end but has no clear end date, and President Gustavo Petro has promised to replace it with a new subsidy to vulnerable households. Although other programs in the region did end as expected after the economic emergency, the lack of political will to retrench on some of the largest emergency programs puts into question the credibility of flexibility even if the programs are originally designed to end along with the emergency.

Better Automatic Stabilizers in Bad Times

Given institutional difficulties in gaining flexibility with government-led transfers, an alternative could be to transfer the deployment and retrenching decision to households. A successful example of this type of transfer is the US Department of Agriculture's Supplemental Nutrition Assistance Program (SNAP), which is the United States' largest food assistance program. In fiscal year 2018, SNAP served an average 40.3 million people per month and issued US$60.9 billion in benefits to be spent in food stores authorized to accept SNAP benefits. The primary goal of SNAP is to provide low-income households with additional resources for buying food. But SNAP also serves as an automatic stabilizer for the economy and, different from CCTs, the deployment timing depends on the household. Food assistance is available for only a limited amount of uses throughout the life of the beneficiary. This design forces households to optimize when and how much to use these benefits. This means that the incentives are placed so that benefits would be best deployed during the worst of the crisis and will automatically retrench as households regain access to regular income. Evidence in the United States shows SNAP to be an effective complement to UI and an important automatic stabilizer during economic downturns.[5]

Protecting Public Investment and Pensions Is Key to Securing Long-Term Inclusive Growth

Although a combination of BBRs and ERs address issues of long-term sustainability and opens fiscal space for countercyclical policies, concerns remain about the effect of these rules on the composition of spending. Two compositional biases, public investment and pensions, are especially concerning.

Investment-Friendly Rules Supported by More Fiscal Space in Good Times

ERs can reduce spending overruns in good times, but they can also lead to stricter prioritization, which, added to political economy arguments, may result in the crowding out of productive but electorally unappealing projects (Debrun 2014). The procyclicality of public investment, especially in bad times, causes serious concerns for long-term growth in low- and middle-income countries.

Public investment bias seems to originate mainly from political economy arguments, such as the length of time policy makers have left in their term before the next election and the fact that there is no constituency now for benefits that may materialize in a decade. In the presence of short political time horizons, fiscal asymmetrical responses with a bias against public investment and toward current spending grow depending on the political payoffs of each spending component. Including well-defined, investment-friendly rules or clauses in ERs can help mitigate public investment bias. In fact, many low- and middle-income markets already have such provisions in different shapes. Brazil, for example, requires by constitutional mandate that credit operations (including financial revenues) cannot exceed capital expenditures (including amortizations). In Peru, expenditure on maintenance of infrastructure, goods and services of social programs covered by the performance-based budgeting scheme, and equipment intended for public order and security were excluded from current ER.

In any case, these compositional rules aiming to defend public investment from being adjusted might just come too late. When fiscal consolidations need to be imposed, a legitimate concern to shield social spending during downturns to protect those who are most vulnerable can compromise the compliance of investment-friendly rules. However, governments are concerned with maximizing the intertemporal welfare of their citizens, and, if public investment is cut to finance present transfers, there is a clear trade-off between welfare today and welfare tomorrow. Arguably, politics dictates that the future is excessively discounted, and only a system of rules can mitigate that.

To ensure effectiveness of these rules, we first need to ensure the retraction elasticity of social spending after a crisis so that other components of spending, such as public investment, are not permanently crowded out.

Formula-Based Indexation to Protect Pensions

In contrast with high-income economies, this report shows that social security is procyclical in the low- and middle-income countries. Procyclicality in social security means higher macroeconomic volatility, but, most important, it means cutting benefits to the most vulnerable individuals when they most need them.

The puzzle surrounding the automatic spending procyclicality in low- and middle-income countries stems from the reliance on policy makers' ad hoc or discretionary criteria in making funding decisions.

This means, on the one hand, that individual social security benefits payments tend to be linked to the revenue capacity of the social security system, which, by its very nature, comoves positively with output. This imparts an upward bias in this spending. On the other hand, although important pension system reforms across low- and middle-income markets have long been needed, typically adjusting for longer life expectancy and unrealistic promises of payouts, pensions are a commitment across the lifetime of the individual, and the real value of the promised payout should be guaranteed.

A possible solution to this problem, in the context of reforms making systems sustainable, could be the effective implementation of formula-based indexation mechanisms typically linked to changes in the cost of living, such as prices or nominal wages, to determine social security payments. This could be achieved, as in most high-income countries, by having inflation-based adjusted formulas that help maintain the real purchasing power of those transfers. Using temporary patches by reducing the real value of a pension not only does not solve the inherent unsustainability of many pension systems in the region but is also highly regressive and recessive for a largely vulnerable group in low- and middle-income nations.

Another potential solution could involve a system that removes the ability to make ad hoc or discretionary changes in pension funding from the policy maker's hands, allowing the private sector to manage the system, with Chile being the archetypical example. Unfortunately, the Chilean system, once considered a gold standard, is now facing criticism and doubts about its survival. Initially praised and emulated worldwide, the current structure of the system is deemed to be flawed. The system's five investment funds have encountered issues with risk-adjusted returns, with the riskier funds not adequately compensating participants. Regulations discouraging investments in alternative assets and mandating currency hedging have further affected returns. Contributory challenges, including low contribution rates, informal labor market participation, and a lack of understanding among workers, have led to disappointing pensions. Proposed reforms by the government are seen by some as potential threats to the existing system. Suggested reforms for countries choosing to privately manage their pension systems following the Chilean example include eliminating investment limits by asset class, adopting a risk-based investment policy at the portfolio level, relaxing restrictions on alternative investments, and revising ill-designed hedge requirements (see Cifuentes 2023; Evans and Pienknagura 2021).

Using the Cyclical Squeeze as an Impetus to Efficiency Savings

Although procyclical behavior of public consumption in good times joined with downward rigidity in bad times must lead to fiscal deficits, the sustainability of such deficits in part depends on the economic returns gained from such spending. This is because fiscal sustainability is typically measured as the ability of a country to meet its debt obligations and, thus, depends on both the size of the obligations and the country's income. Because there are potentially large marginal returns on education, health, and public safety, low- and middle-income markets should be able to sustain larger public deficits as long as these generate economic growth. Unfortunately, the provision of public goods in low- and middle-income nations is often highly inefficient, and thus the promised returns may not materialize. Although institutional determinants of inefficient spending, such as lack of capabilities, negligence, and corruption, are deeply rooted in all public institutions across low- and middle-income countries and will take time and effort to improve, there is low-hanging fruit in efficiency gains that can be used not only to improve fiscal space in the short run but also to contribute to growth down the road.

To identify efficiency-enhancing and readily available policy options, a better use of data can help design better public policies (World Bank 2021c). Ample data and analysis can be found in the *Handbook of Government Analytics: An Empirical Guide to Measurement in Public Administration* (Rogger and Schuster 2023). For example, the World Bank regularly undertakes reviews of procurement practices and simulations of possible savings. For three countries in LAC, savings of 16–22 percent were estimated on purchases with straightforward modifications of practices and without changing existing procurement laws. In one country, savings of 7 percent of purchases were estimated purely from consolidating purchases across government (bulk buying); 2.5 percent, from the use of electronic catalogs, better use of reverse auctions, and avoiding noncompetitive contracts; 1.3 percent, from more timely processing of contracts; and 1 percent, from avoiding seasonal bunching of procurement. Indirectly eliminating barriers to bidding on government contracts and, hence, increasing the number of bidders was estimated to generate potential savings of 2.4 percent, and developing special procedures for especially concentrated markets, another 1.8 percent. Other studies show how improving the quality of procurement specialists from the bottom 20th percentile to the median could represent 10 percent of savings in public spending.

Efficiency in public consumption can also be gained in the short run by rethinking spending priorities. A recent report from the World Bank (2021b) lists several ways to redirect spending that could lead to important efficiency and productivity gains in the near future. Among those related to the provision of public goods, the report highlights the need to strengthen health and education systems in low- and middle-income countries. Better public health systems would greatly improve productivity through a healthier labor force. Solutions for more effective education systems may be different at different levels of education. For primary and secondary schools, governments should prioritize funding for the hardest-hit schools and communities and explore the potential for using resources more efficiently. Additionally, the adoption of several innovations in education, the most important of which may be the use of technology, could help provide effective tools for online teaching, flexibility, and adaptability to teach at the right level and help implement early warning systems based on students' attendance patterns to prevent them from falling behind or dropping out. Technology can also allow better allocation of resources across different students and communities. For higher education, middle-income regions such as LAC display bloated spending on higher education relative to comparator countries. This spending is typically inequitably distributed and does not provide the needed skills for rapid growth. Taking relatively inexpensive actions to increase transparency and accountability and explore the reallocation of public higher education funding among students, programs, institutions, and fields would be a step in the right direction, from both a growth and an equity perspective.

Notes

1. The literature finds that multiyear structural fiscal rules can help governments implement countercyclical fiscal policy if they include proper escape clauses (see Ayuso-i-Casals et al. 2009; Bergman and Hutchison 2015; Bova, Carcenac, and Guerguil 2014; Combes et al. 2014). Beetsma et al. (2019) and Reuter (2019) show, in the context of the European Union country members, that the presence of a fiscal council is positively correlated with higher compliance with fiscal rules.

2. See Herrera and Olaberria (2020) for a more detailed discussion.

3. As noted in Larraín et al. (2019), tasks are still pending completion in the implementation of fiscal rules in Chile. These include restoring the structural balance, explicitly defining escape clauses and criteria for returning to the target, making the calculation of structural parameters less procyclical, strengthening institutional behavior in the operation of expert committees, improving reporting and fiscal transparency, and enhancing medium- and long-term public financial planning.

4. Among large economies in the LAC, only Argentina did not have a balanced budget rule before the pandemic; it was dropped in 2017.

5. See Hoynes and Schanzenbach (2019) and Finifter and Prell (2013) for highlights of the role of the Supplemental Nutrition Assistance Program as an effective automatic stabilizer.

References

Alesina, A. F., and T. Bayoumi. 1996. "The Costs and Benefits of Fiscal Rules: Evidence from U.S States." Working Paper 5614, National Bureau of Economic Research, Cambridge, MA.

Ayuso-i-Casals, J. 2012. *National Expenditure Rules: Why, How and When*. Economic Papers 473. Brussels: European Commission, Directorate-General for Economic and Financial Affairs.

Ayuso-i-Casals, J., D. G. Hernandez, L. Moulin, and A. Turrini. 2009. "Beyond the SGP: Features and Effects of EU National-Level Numerical Fiscal Rules." In *Instruments for Sound Fiscal Policies*, edited by J. Ayuso-i-Casals, S. Deroose, E. Flores, and L. Moulin, 204–40. London: Palgrave Macmillan. https://doi.org/10.1057/9780230271791_10.

Beetsma, R., X. Debrun, X. Fang, Y. Kim, V. Lledó, S. Mbaye, and X. Zhang. 2019. "Independent Fiscal Councils: Recent Trends and Performance." *European Journal of Political Economy* 57: 53–69.

Bergman, U. M., and M. Hutchison. 2015. "Economic Stabilization in the Post-Crisis World: Are Fiscal Rules the Answer?" *Journal of International Money and Finance* 52: 82–101.

Blanchard, O. J., and F. Giavazzi. 2004. "Improving the SGP through a Proper Accounting of Public Investment." Discussion Paper 4220, Centre for Economic Policy Research, London.

Blanco, F., P. Saavedra, F. Koehler-Geib, and E. Skrok, eds. 2020. *Fiscal Rules and Economic Size in Latin America and the Caribbean.* Washington, DC: World Bank.

Bouwen, P. 2009. "The European Commission." In *Lobbying the European Union: Institutions, Actors, and Issues,* edited by D. Coen and J. Richardson, 19–38. Oxford: Oxford University Press.

Bova, M. E., N. Carcenac, and M. M. Guerguil. 2014. "Fiscal Rules and the Procyclicality of Fiscal Policy in the Developing World." Working Paper WP/14/122, International Monetary Fund, Washington, DC.

Cifuentes, A. 2023. "Chile's Pioneering Pension System Now Needs Reform." *Financial Times,* December 28, 2023. https://www.ft.com/content/7f2c2d17-8b47-4ad3-bf9a-6e342e6d66c6.

Clemens, J., and S. Miran. 2012. "Fiscal Policy Multipliers on Subnational Government Spending." *American Economic Journal: Economic Policy* 4 (2): 46–68.

Combes, J. L., M. X. Debrun, A. Minea, and R. Tapsoba. 2014. "Inflation Targeting and Fiscal Rules: Do Interactions and Sequencing Matter?" Working Paper WP/14/89, International Monetary Fund, Washington, DC.

Cordes, T., M. T. Kinda, M. P. S. Muthoora, and A. Weber. 2015. "Expenditure Rules: Effective Tools for Sound Fiscal Policy?" Working Paper WP/15/29, International Monetary Fund, Washington, DC.

Davoodi, H. D, P. Elger, A. Fotiou, D. Garcia-Macia, A. Lagerborg, R. Lam, and S. Pillai. 2022. "Fiscal Councils Dataset: The 2021 Update." Washington, DC: International Monetary Fund.

Debrun, X. 2014. "How Expenditure Rules Can Help Get Public Spending Right." *IMF PFM Blog.* June 30, 2014. https://blog-pfm.imf.org/en/pfmblog/2014/06/how-expenditure-rules-can-help-public-spending-right.html.

Debrun, X., T. Kinda, T. Curristine, L. Eyraud, J. Harris, and J. Seiwald. 2013. "The Functions and Impact of Fiscal Councils." IMF Policy Paper, International Monetary Fund, Washington, DC.

Debrun, X., L. Moulin, A. Turrini, J. Ayuso-i-Casals, and M. S. Kumar. 2008. "Tied to the Mast? National Fiscal Rules in the European Union." *Economic Policy* 23 (54): 298–362.

Defensoria Pública da União. 2021. "DPU: Dados Auxílio Emergencial." https://www.dpu.def.br/.

Espino, E., and J. M. Sanchez. 2013. "Unemployment Insurance in High Informality Countries." Working Paper WP-403, Inter-American Development Bank, Washington, DC.

Evans, C., and S. Pienknagura. 2021. "Assessing Chile's Pension System: Challenges and Reform Options." IMF Working Paper, International Monetary Fund, Washington, DC.

Eyraud, L., M. X. Debrun, A. Hodge, V. D. Lledo, and M. C. A. Pattillo. 2018. *Second-Generation Fiscal Rules: Balancing Simplicity, Flexibility, and Enforceability.* IMF Staff Discussion Note SDN/18/04, International Monetary Fund, Washington, DC.

Fall, F., D. Bloch, J. M. Fournier, and P. Hoeller. 2015. "Prudent Debt Targets and Fiscal Frameworks." Economic Policy Paper No. 15, Organisation for Economic Co-operation and Development, Paris.

Fatás, A., and I. Mihov. 2006. "The Macroeconomic Effects of Fiscal Rules in the US States." *Journal of Public Economics* 90 (1–2): 101–17.

Finifter, D. H., and M. A. Prell. 2013. *Participation in the Supplemental Nutrition Assistance Program (SNAP) and Unemployment Insurance: How Tight Are the Strands of the Recessionary Safety Net?* Economic Research Report No. ERR-157. Washington, DC: U.S. Department of Agriculture, Economic Research Service.

Heinemann, M., and M. Yeter. 2018. "Do Fiscal Rules Constrain Fiscal Policy? A Meta-Regression-Analysis." *European Journal of Political Economy* 51: 69–92.

Herrera, S., and E. Olaberria. 2020. *Budget Rigidity in Latin America and the Caribbean: Causes, Consequences, and Policy Implications.* International Development in Focus. Washington, DC: World Bank.

Hoynes, H., and D. Schanzenbach. 2019. "Strengthening SNAP as an Automatic Stabilizer." In *Recession Ready: Fiscal Policies to Stabilize the American Economy*, edited by H. Boushey, R. Nunn, and J. Shambaugh, 217–36. Washington, DC: Brookings Institute.

Iara, A., and G. B. Wolff. 2014. "Rules and Risks in the Euro Area." *European Journal of Political Economy* 34: 222–36.

International Monetary Fund. 2013. *The Functions and Impact of Fiscal Councils.* Washington, DC: International Monetary Fund.

Larraín, F., L. A. Ricci, K. Schmidt-Hebbel, H. González, M. Hadzi-Vaskov, and A. Pérez, eds. 2019. *Enhancing Chile's Fiscal Framework: Lessons from Domestic and International Experience.* Washington, DC: International Monetary Fund.

Marneffe, W., B. Aarle, W. Wielen, and L. Vereeck. 2011. "The Impact of Fiscal Rules on Public Finances in the Euro Area." *CESifo DICE Report* 9 (3): 18–26.

Reuter, W. H. 2019. "When and Why Do Countries Break Their National Fiscal Rules?" *European Journal of Political Economy* 57: 125–41.

Rogger, D., and C. Schuster, eds. 2023. *The Government Analytics Handbook: Leveraging Data to Strengthen Public Administration.* Washington, DC: World Bank.

Valencia, O., and C. Ulloa-Suarez. 2022. "Do Governments Stick to Their Announced Fiscal Rules? A Study of Latin American and the Caribbean Countries." *Journal of Government and Economics* 8: 1000058.

World Bank. 2021a. *Auxílio Emergencial—Lessons from the Brazilian Experience Responding to COVID-19.* Washington, DC: World Bank. https://doi.org/10.1596/37254.

World Bank. 2021b. *Recovering Growth: Rebuilding Dynamic Post-COVID-19 Economies amid Fiscal Constraints.* LAC Semiannual Report. Washington, DC: World Bank.

World Bank. 2021c. *World Development Report 2021: Data for Better Lives.* Washington, DC: World Bank.

Wyplosz, C. 2013. "Europe's Quest for Fiscal Discipline." Economic Papers 498, European Commission, Brussels.